English Solutions

Book 3

Driven to th...

In 1990, almost 40% of people involved
under 17. Recent studies have shown t
joyriders start taking cars between the
passengers as young as 10 years of age
people break the law in this way and pu
innocent people in such danger?

In this unit you will think about
issues as you '

The Harry
Hastings method

most popular novels, television series and films
with crime. Often, books are *adapted* as films
ms are published in book form.

read and discuss a crime
closely at the way the
to make you.

It's the way
that yo...

English
Solutions
Book 3

Jim Sweetman

Shelagh Hubbard

John Mannion

Contents

The activities in this book have been coded by colour, according to the *main* skill used in them. This coding is for ease of reference and does not imply that this skill is the sole focus of the activity: an activity coded a 'reading' activity may involve writing, and a 'speaking & listening' activity may often emerge from a reading activity and lead into a written outcome.

●	= Speaking & Listening
●	= Reading
●	= Writing

Unit title and core activity	Development of key skills	Assignment	Key skills/tips	Cross-curricular options
1. Listen up! Exploring and improving listening skills through activity and discussion. Reading *Men Talk* by Liz Lochhead	● Listen carefully and positively ● Reach conclusions through discussions ● Respond and restructure ● Structure talks for an audience ● Write in non-literary ways	Answering quiz on listening skills Role playing scenes Interviewing a friend Observing discussion	Tips: Better listening Tips: Open, closed and interesting questions Tips: Observing talk Tips: Better class discussions	Links to development of oral skills in other subjects, e.g. the questionnaire could be modified to suit other subject requirements
2. CD covers Discussing aspects of media and promotion through an analysis of the design of CD covers	● Contribute in discussion ● Engage with content and language ● Respond to factual and informative texts ● Write in non-literary ways ● Use presentational devices	Ranking reasons for buying audiotapes and CDs Noting information on a typical CD cover Designing a box cover		Links to media studies, art, design and technology
3. Animal characters Exploring the presentation of animals in extracts from Aesop's *Fables*, Chaucer's *The Nun's Priest's Tale*, *The Second Jungle Book* by Rudyard Kipling, *Black Beauty* by Anna Sewell and *White Fang* by Jack London	● Contribute in discussion ● Read narrative ● Write narrative	Discussion of fables Reading, discussing and commenting in writing on extracts Role playing a discussion by writers Writing an animal story		
4. Design and presentation Presentation approached through poems where shape or text effects are major features. Including Apollinaire, Dylan Thomas, George Herbert and modern poets	● Respond and restructure ● Read poetry ● Write poetry ● Use presentational devices	Identifying presentational effects in a selection of poems Using texts effects to present prose extracts as poems Writing a poem that uses similes	Skills: Understanding what a poem looks like Skills: Aspects of presentation Tips: Experimenting with DTP and graphics	This unit will benefit from access to computers and close links to word-processing and DTP use elsewhere in the curriculum
5. Shakespeare & his theatre An exploration of how extracts from *Julius Caesar*, *A Midsummer Night's Dream* and *Romeo and Juliet* might have been staged at the Globe Theatre	● Reach conclusions through discussion ● Write in non-literary ways ● Write narrative	Answering questions on the staging of *Julius Caesar*, *A Midsummers Night's Dream* and *Romeo and Juliet* Writing empathically about a visit to the Globe Theatre		Links to drama

Unit title and core activity	Development of key skills	Assignment	Key skills/tips	Cross-curricular options
6. The Harry Hastings method Reading and analysing a short story, *The Harry Hastings Method* by Warner Law	• Reach conclusions through discussion • Understand the development of language • Read narrative • Engage with content and language	Using clues to predict the ending of a short story Analysing aspects of the writer's style Adapting a short story for television	Tips: Adapting for television	Links to media studies
7. It's the way that you say It A detailed discussion of accents and dialects. Reading two extracts featuring dialect by Gloria Cook and Liselle Kayla	• Understand the development of language • Listen carefully and positively • Structure talk for an audience • Read narrative • Read plays • Write script	Discussing contexts where talk may vary Writing a personal language history Reading and discussing extracts Writing a script	Skills: Spoken English Tips: Setting out a script Tips: Writing dialogue that reflects dialect	Links to cross-curriculum language and PSE
8. Good friends A discussion of friendship based on extracts from *Tom Sawyer* by Mark Twain, *Jane Eyre* by Charlotte Brontë and *The Red Ball* by Ismith Khan	• Listen carefully and positively • Restructure and respond • Read narrative • Write narrative	Discussing what makes a good friend Answering questions on extracts Writing about a character in one of the extracts studied		
9. Driven to the limits Exploring the issue of car theft by juveniles. Writing a realistic short story based on factual evidence	• Reach conclusions through discussion • Respond to factual and informative texts • Write narrative • Understand the writing process	Discussing why cars are stolen by young people Creating a character Developing plot and subplot and making decisions about viewpoint	Tips: Plots and sub-plots Skills: Narrative viewpoints Tips: How to write endings	
10. Animal crackers Research and study of an animal rights issue leading to an analysis of persuasive writing. Writing a magazine article	• Contribute in discussion • Engage with content and language • Write in non-literary ways • Understand and use standard English	Discussion and research on a range of activities involving animals Writing a formal letter to ask for information Analysing the style of two pieces of persuasive writing Writing an article	Tips: Getting started when you want to find out information Tips: Writing letters to find out information Skills: Researching an issue	

Listen up!

Are you a good listener? Whether you are or not, it is always possible to improve your listening skills and to show other people that you really are listening to – and *hearing* – what they are saying.

 In this unit you will answer questions to see how well you listen. You will look at ways to improve your listening skills and interview a partner.

Check how well you listen

Check your listening habits by doing the quiz on this page.

Make a note of which answer is true for you. Be honest!

1   You are talking with a group of your friends during your lunch break at school.
Do you:
a   Entertain everyone with stories about things that have happened to you?
b   Say nothing and just listen?
c   Respond to the others by asking questions and making comments?
d   Spend lunchtime alone, because most of the people in your school are boring?

2   You are in a lesson where the teacher is giving a detailed explanation to the class.
Do you:
a   Keep quiet and think about something more interesting?
b   Interrupt the teacher from time to time by asking about points you don't understand, or which you would like repeated?
c   Carry on a whispered conversation with a friend about your private life?
d   Keep quiet and hope the work you do afterwards will help you understand?

3   You are having a class discussion in an English lesson.
Do you:
a   Join in to agree with others, or to point out reasons why you feel some of their points are not quite accurate?
b   Sit in silence and think about something else?
c   Make sure everyone knows exactly what you think, and join in with witty comments?
d   Sit in silence and think about what you would like to say, if you had the confidence?

4   You are in a small group doing a science experiment.
Do you:
a   Tell everyone else what to do?
b   Make sure everyone in the group gets the chance to join in the discussion by checking that everyone agrees with the conclusions you write down?
c   Do what the others tell you?
d   Let the others get on with it and think about something more interesting?

5   Your friend is telling you how to get to a higher level on a new computer game.
Do you:
a   Interrupt and tell him or her a way you think would be better?
b   Listen quietly and agree with everything?
c   Stay quiet and wish your friend wasn't so obsessed with computers?
d   Ask questions and make comments which show you are interested in the new method?

6   **In your English lesson someone is giving a talk about his or her hobby.**
    Do you:

    a   Sit in silence and think about something else?

    b   Make an effort to listen to enough of the talk to help you think up a few interesting questions to ask at the end?

    c   Carry on a conversation with your friend, only stopping to ask questions you hope will embarrass the presenter of the talk?

    d   Sit quietly and wonder how he or she got interested in the hobby in the first place?

7   **Your drama teacher has put you in a group of people you don't really get on with.**
    Do you:

    a   Say nothing and let them get on with it?

    b   Argue with them about absolutely everything and refuse to work with them unless they do what you say?

    c   Do what they tell you?

    d   Join in as well as you can, agreeing where you feel able to and asking questions if you feel the group should consider different ideas?

8   **A guest speaker has come to talk to your class about a career which isn't something you would want to do.**
    Do you:

    a   Sit quietly and spend most of the time imagining yourself landing your dream job and amazing everyone by how good you are at it?

    b   Take an interest in what the speaker is saying and think of a couple of questions to ask him or her about what the job involves?

    c   Think about your plans for the next school holiday?

    d   Carry on a conversation with your friend in the back row – and sometimes with others sitting near you as well?

9   **A friend is talking to you about something which has really upset him or her.**
    Do you:

    a   Make him or her feel better by talking about something even worse that happened to you and explaining how you got over it?

    b   Feel embarrassed, say nothing and hope that your friend gets it out of his or her system quickly?

    c   Ask a few questions to make sure your friend has told you everything he or she wants, then make a few comments to show you understand how he or she feels and offer some advice?

    d   Listen in silence, not feeling too sure what you should say?

10 **Your parent is telling you off about the state of your bedroom, the cost of your phone calls, the time you came in last night, etc.**
    Do you:

    a   Say 'yes' and 'no' when it seems appropriate?

    b   Listen carefully to his or her point of view, and promise to improve?

    c   Complain that you are being picked on and storm off?

    d   Listen in silence and feel deeply misunderstood?

How to work out your score

Each answer is worth 0, 1, 2 or 3 marks. Add up the total score for your answers.

	1	2	3	4	5	6	7	8	9	10
a	3	0	2	3	3	0	0	1	3	1
b	1	2	0	2	1	2	3	2	0	3
c	2	3	3	1	0	3	1	0	2	2
d	0	1	1	0	2	1	2	3	1	0

How did you score?

0–7

You probably think you are a really good listener because you don't say very much – but sitting in silence isn't the same thing as listening. Half the time you are just as likely to be day-dreaming or staring out of the window. Try living in the real world! You might find it interesting.

8–15

You might be a good listener, but it's difficult for anyone to tell, because you don't let them know that you are listening. You're not very confident about speaking out in large groups – and maybe you're a bit lazy too. You find it easier to let others do the talking.

16–22

You know what listening is all about: you get involved in what people are saying by commenting on what you hear and asking questions about it, rather than competing with others to say the most. You are also aware that some people need to be encouraged to talk and that others need to be told to be quiet at times to let them get a word in.

23–25

You are reasonable at listening when you are interested, or when you get on with the group you are talking to, but you really prefer to talk. You need to be more aware of other people: give the quiet ones some encouragement – and don't be so quick to disagree before you have found out the reasons for what others say.

26–30

Basically, you like the sound of your own voice. You are probably super-confident and a good talker, but you are very selfish about giving anyone else a chance. You need to learn how to listen.

2 How to improve your listening skills

Study the hints on how to be a better listener in the Tips box on the next page. With a partner, choose one or two of the following situations:

- Two neighbours chat across the garden fence.
- A boss and a worker talk about tea breaks.
- A shop assistant is helpful or unhelpful.
- A teacher talks to a pupil about an incident on the bus.

Working from one of these situations, improvise the 'perfect' conversation, taking account of all the suggestions in the Tips box.

Then, improvise a scene where these suggestions are ignored.

Show your improvisations to the class.

3 Interview a friend

Choose a partner you do not often talk to. If possible, choose someone of the opposite sex. Take it in turns to interview each other and note down the answers to your questions.

To make the interview go well, try the following:

 Help your partner relax before you start. It isn't always easy to talk about yourself to someone you do not know very well.

- Start with some straightforward questions.
- Don't always be satisfied with a quick answer. If necessary, ask your partner to explain the reasons for a reply.
- Make sure you practise your listening techniques during the interview.
- Remember to thank your partner at the end of the interview.

... on how to be a better listener

1 Use body language

Make eye-contact with the person who is speaking.

Face them. Lean towards them.

Nod and shake your head to show agreement or disagreement.

Show by your expression that you are interested, amused, shocked or puzzled.

2 Show that you've listened

Use words to encourage the speaker: 'mm', 'yes', 'I should think not!'

Ask for details and explanations.

Ask others in the group if they agree or disagree with what has been said.

Put ideas into your own words in order to check what has been said. Rephrase, summarise.

Tell people to be quiet and listen to less confident speakers.

3 Respond to what you have heard

Don't interrupt or change the subject.

Explain the reasons for your own different points of view. Ask whether others agree.

Be prepared to adapt what you believe to take account of what others say.

... on the difference between open, closed and interesting questions

Closed questions

These questions produce factual or simple answers which do not move the conversation forward. Here are some examples of closed questions:

How old are you?
Where do you live?
What lessons do you like?

Open questions

These give the person being interviewed a chance to say more and to give his or her personal opinion. These are examples of open questions:

What do you think about where you live?
What are your views on assemblies?

Interesting questions

A good test of a question is to think how you would answer it if it was put to you. Would you have to pause and reflect or could you reply without thinking? An interesting question forces you to think before answering.

Magazine and television interviews are good places to look out for interesting questions.

How would *you* answer these open questions?

–   When and where were you happiest?
–   What words or phrases do you use too much?
–   How do you like to relax?
–   What characteristic do you most dislike in adults?
–   What is your nastiest habit?
–   Where would you like to be in ten years' time?
–   Where do you *think* you will be?
–   How would you define a real friend?
–   If you were a teacher, what would you be like?
–   Would you ever play truant from school?

4 Find out if girls and boys talk differently

For the next task, you need to start with a friend of your own sex.

Read this poem by Liz Lochhead.

Men Talk
(Rap)

Women
Rabbit rabbit rabbit women
Tattle and titter
Women prattle
Women waffle and witter

Men Talk. Men Talk.

Women into Girl Talk
About Women's Trouble
Trivial 'n Small Talk
They yap and they babble

Men Talk. Men Talk.

Women gossip Women giggle
Women niggle-niggle-niggle
Men Talk.

Women yatter
Women chatter
Women chew the fat, women spill the beans
Women aint been takin'
The oh-so Good Advice in them
Women's Magazines.

A Man Likes A Good Listener.

Oh yeah
I like A Woman
Who likes me enough
Not to nitpick
Not to nag and
Not to interrupt 'cause I call that treason
A woman with the Good Grace
To be struck dumb
By me Sweet Reason. Yes —

A Man Likes A Good Listener.

A Real
Man
Likes a Real Good Listener

Women yap, yap, yap
Verbal Diarrhoea is a Female Disease
Woman she spread she rumours round she
Like Philadelphia Cream Cheese

Oh
Bossy Women Gossip
Girlish Women Giggle
Women natter, women nag
Women niggle niggle niggle

Men Talk

Men
Think First, Speak Later
Men Talk.

Liz Lochhead

How do you react to the poem?

Would your reaction be different if you were the opposite sex?

The list of statements below is taken from a report by school inspectors. The inspectors express their concern about what sometimes happens when school pupils are speaking and listening in mixed classes.

Read the statements through.

Boys' and girls' talk: what the inspectors saw

- In lessons, boys dominate, answering more questions, offering more opinions and interrupting more frequently than girls.

- Teachers pay more attention to boys, especially when boys sit in the centre of the room and become the focus for the teacher's attention.

- In pairs and groups, boys are more likely than girls to interrupt one another, argue openly and voice opinions strongly.

- When boys and girls work together in mixed groups, some of them find it embarrassing or find it more difficult to get the work done than in single sex groups.

- Some boys, and even more girls, lack confidence about talking in groups bigger than a pair, especially joining in with whole-class discussion.

Take it in turns to explain to each other whether you think the inspectors' statements (on the previous page) are true or false. Give examples from your own experience to explain your opinions.

Decide whether you think each statement is mostly true, sometimes true, or mostly untrue.

... on watching talk

1 **Remember to practise your listening techniques**

2 **Whatever happens, keep silent**
The person you are observing will try to draw you into the discussion – particularly if he or she is embarrassed!

3 **The best position for observing is sitting slightly behind and to the side of the person you are watching**
In this position you can watch the person's body language and listen to what people say without getting in the way of the discussion group.

Join with another pair, of the opposite sex, to make a mixed group of four.

For this activity, you will be discussing these statements and seeing which you agree with. You will also spend some of your time observing another person to see whether the statements *are* true.

Pair up with another group, so that you now have two groups of four. One group will observe the other group as they discuss these statements.

Decide who is going to observe whom (if you can observe someone of the opposite sex, that might be an interesting experiment). Then, decide which group of four will talk first.

Use a copy of the observation sheet below to help you record what the person you are watching does. Put a tick (or a brief comment) each time you notice him or her doing one of the things listed on the chart.

Swap over after about ten minutes. The group that was discussing now observes; the group that was observing now discusses the statements.

Observer sheet about (Name)

Discussing (Topic)

Observed by (Name)

Date

Observer's comments

Supportive listening

Eye contact	Body position	Expression	Encouraging words	Asking for explanation	Involving others	Rephrasing/ summarising

Competitive talking

Interrupting	Offering new opinions – and repeating them	Arguing/disagreeing	Ignoring other people's contributions

Observee's comments

5 Compare your findings

Now, let the whole class share what your group found out. You will need to report back on two things:

- the conclusions you reached in your discussion groups

- the information you gathered from your observations – and whether these support or contradict the opinions you have been discussing.

Draw up a list of ten class rules which will help everyone to listen better during discussion work – and display them on your classroom wall.

TIPS ...

... on better class discussions

1 Use your listening techniques
You need them most of all in a large group discussion.

2 Don't interrupt other speakers
Only one person should be speaking at a time. If you want to make a point, wait for your turn: follow the rules about raising your hand, or waiting for the teacher to invite your opinion.

3 Allow others to speak
If someone who rarely talks in class discussions puts forward an interesting point in your group, ask him or her to explain it to the class rather than saying it yourself.

4 Try to give everyone the chance to say something

on target

After working through this unit, could you:

- show you were a better listener during group work in class?

- explain to a friend how a good listener behaves?

- recognise typically 'male' or 'female' behaviour in discussion?

- make sure you do not behave in a 'typically male' or 'typically female' way yourself when you are speaking and listening?

CD covers

Young people spend about £200 million a year on CDs, roughly a quarter of the total of £800 million spent on CDs in the UK. According to the statistics, almost half of all 16 to 24 year olds bought a CD album or CD single in the last six months, and the figure is rising steadily.

> **In this unit you will look at how the appearance of a CD's box appeals to a particular type of buyer. You will read and discuss the information which goes into the making of a CD cover, then design and write a CD cover for a band of your own choice.**

▮ Choosing CDs

What would make *you* choose a particular CD?

> In a small group, talk about the music you have bought in the last six months. What made you choose those CDs or tapes out of the thousands available?

Record companies design covers that appeal to the people who might want to buy that type of music. The music and the box make up a *package* to attract potential buyers.

> Think about the tape or CD each of you bought most recently. Look at the reasons opposite. Choose five that most closely reflect your reasons for buying the tape or CD. Put them in order of importance, from most to least important.

	Reasons for buying
1	I heard all of the CD before I bought it and liked it very much.
2	I liked the video.
3	It was on special offer.
4	It was advertised on television.
5	I saw it in the shop.
6	I like that band/singer and wanted the new CD.
7	One of my friends had it.
8	I saw the singer or band on television or video.
9	The singer or group is popular/in the charts.
10	It's a 'classic': everyone ought to have it in their collection.
11	I identify with the image of the singer or band.
12	I already have another CD or tape by this singer or band.
13	My parent doesn't like it.
14	The cover design caught my eye.
15	I wanted to impress people and seem mature.
16	I liked the words of the songs.
17	I read a review of it and it sounded good.

> Compare your group's reasons for choosing CDs and tapes with those of the rest of the class. Which reasons are most important in influencing your choices?
>
> - The music itself?
> - The way record companies publicise, advertise and package their products?

2 Look at CD covers

CD singles come in flexible envelopes, while CD albums come in rigid plastic boxes – these are called 'jewel boxes' in the trade. Jewel boxes are made in three sections: they have a back, a lid and a piece of moulded plastic which holds the CD.

The 'insert' slots inside the front of the box and a single sheet fits into the back. The sizes of these inserts vary. Some are booklets while others unfold to make posters.

With your group, look at the four CD covers illustrated on these pages and note down your answers to these questions:

- What information is given on each front cover?

- What does the illustration show?

- Can you tell just by looking at the covers what kind of music each CD contains? What clues help you?

Report your ideas back to the class.

3 Look at the information on a CD

Select one CD of your own and make notes about the cover illustration. Then, take a close look at all the information contained on the box and insert and note down your answers to these questions.

Look at the whole box:
- What is the full title of the CD?
- Who is the CD by?
- Who recorded it? Where?
- What are the song titles?
- Who mixed the music?
- When was it made?
- What is the catalogue number?
- Who are the publishers?

Look at the insert:
- How long is the CD?
- What is on the cover?
- What is inside?
- Are there any pictures?
- How many different 'logos' can you find on the CD? Copy each of them.
- Look at the acknowledgements. How many names are there?
- Are the lyrics enclosed? Who wrote the songs or music? Does the box or insert say how long each song is?
- What other information is there?

Look at the disc:
- Is it coloured in any way?
- What writing does it contain?
- What information is on the disc that is also on the paper packaging?

Finally, discuss with your group or class what part of this information makes you want to buy the CD.

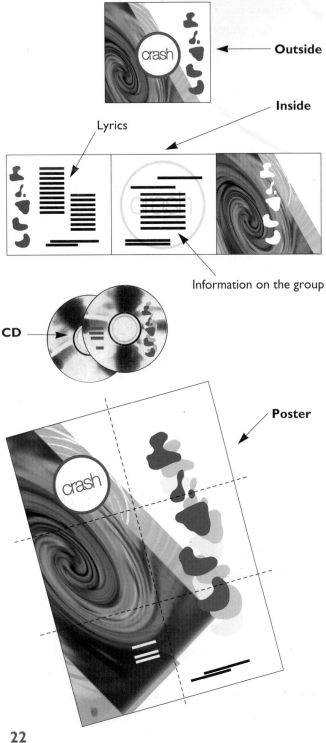

Outside

Inside

Lyrics

Information on the group

CD

Poster

4 Design your own box cover

Now, produce your own CD box cover. You can either do this for an up and coming band which you invent yourself; or you can produce a CD box cover for the band which is described on the page opposite.

If you are inventing your own band, follow these steps for success:

1 Think of your performers and give them a name

Choose a name to reflect their image and music. Then, write a brief description of your chosen band. Include:

- the names and ages of the band members
- how they met
- who plays what
- the music that influenced them
- how they were discovered or became famous
- where the songs on this CD came from, or how they were written.

2 Think of a title for their first album and the tracks it contains

Now start to design your cover insert and the back of the box.
Will you make a booklet, a poster or use a simple folded sheet for your insert?
Decide on the form of the design.

3 Think about the image of your band and the kind of buyer you are trying to attract

Draft out some possible illustrations and talk about them with your group.

What kind of typeface will suit the writing? Would handwriting be better than print? Are you creating the image and giving the message you intend to?

4 Think about the information to include

Decide what will go on the front cover, the back cover and the insert.

5 Now design your final box cover

Will you use a word-processing or DTP package, or should you do some parts of your design with a pen and paper?

Make your design as detailed and attractive as you can.

Make sure that it conveys all of the information required by law, as well as what you want it to say.

Profile of a band

Fungal Infection burst on to the music scene in late 1994 with their second single, 'They came from underground', a hypnotic mixture of lush dance rhythms and raw guitar power. The single reached Number 3 in the Network Top Forty.

Their debut album, *Music from the Forest Floor*, was released to rave reviews in February 1995. The *New Musical Express* described it as 'the authentic voice of disaffected, danced-out Britain in the 90s'. *Smash Hits* called it 'a surprisingly refreshing blast of energy from the young Bristol quartet'.

The band members met at school. They are Frankie 'Death Cap' Thorax (piano and ambient sounds), Chuck 'Fly Agaric' Nelson (percussion and drums), 'Toast' (vocals) and Rosa 'Button' Evans (guitars) – they like to refer to themselves as 'mushrooms 'n' toast'. Based in Bristol, they are fervent vegetarians. They give as their musical influences Public Enemy, Pink Floyd, Abba and Marvin Gaye.

5 Choose a class top ten

Arrange all the covers produced by the class. Carry out a survey.

Find out from each member of your class:
- which three of these CDs he or she would buy
- which three covers he or she thinks are most effective.

Did the members of your class vote for the same CDs in each case, or did they have different answers?

Draw up a class top ten to show the results of your poll.

After working through this unit, could you:

- design another cover for an art or technology project?
- talk about what makes an effective CD cover?
- analyse how a CD cover appeals to the buyer?

Animal characters

We all enjoy reading animal stories at some time in our lives.
Some of the first books we read as children tell stories about
animals, and there are many books, for both older children
and adults, where the main characters are not people, but
animals.

**In this unit you will explore how animals have
been used in literature since ancient times.**

Making animals into people

Many folk tales, myths and legends that feature animals use them to say something about people. We may not find out much about animals from these stories, but we can find out about the people who wrote them and their readers.

The following story is well over 2000 years old and was written by a freed slave named Aesop. This type of story is known as a *fable* – a fable is a story that could not really happen and that often contains a message, or a moral, for the reader.

The hare and the tortoise

A Hare was one day making fun of a Tortoise for being so slow upon his feet. 'Wait a bit,' said the Tortoise; 'I'll run a race with you, and I'll wager that I win.' 'Oh, well,' replied the Hare, who was much amused at the idea, 'let's try and see'; and it was soon agreed that the Fox should set a course for them, and be the judge. When the time came, both started off together, but the Hare was soon so far ahead that he thought he might as well have a rest; so down he lay and fell fast asleep. Meanwhile the Tortoise kept plodding on, and in time reached the goal. At last the Hare woke up with a start, and dashed on at his fastest, but only to find that the Tortoise had already won the race.

Moral: Slow and steady wins the race.

Aesop

People have continued to tell and read this fable over a long period of time, so it must appeal to both adults and children.

Work with your partner and discuss what the reasons for this story's success might be. Note down your answers to these questions:

a   If the fable was about two people, would the behaviour described have been believable?

b   Does the fable tell us anything at all about real hares and real tortoises?

c   What impression is the reader given of the characters of the two animals?

d   Which character do you think children identify with? Why?

e   Which aspect of the fable do you think might please an adult?

Chaucer's English

Below is the retelling of another, longer, fable. It was written in England over 500 years ago as one of the stories told by a group of people going on a pilgrimage to the holy shrine at Canterbury. These stories, called *The Canterbury Tales*, are among the first examples of stories written in English. The man telling the story of Chanticleer, the cockerel, is called the Nun's Priest.

The Canterbury Tales were written by Geoffrey Chaucer. The text you will be reading here is a modern version of one of the tales. The original was written in a form of English you would find strange and difficult to decipher. Below is the opening of the story, as it appears in Chaucer's original version (on the left) and in a modern translation (on the right):

The nun's priest's tale

The Nonnes Preestes Tale

Heere bigynneth the Nonnes Preestes Tale of the Cok and Hen, Chauntecleer and Pertelote.

A povre wydwe, somdeel stape in age
Was whilom dwellyng in a narwe cotage,
Biside a grove, stondynge in a dale.
This wydwe, of which I telle yow my tale,
Syn thilke day that she was last a wyf,
In pacience ladde a ful symple lyf,
For litel was hir catel and hir rente.
By housbondrie of swich as God hire sente
She foond hirself and eek hir doghtren two.
Thre large sowes hadde she, and namo,
Three keen, and eek a sheep that highte Malle.
Ful sooty was hire bour and eek hir halle,
In which she eet ful many a sklendre meel.

Once, long ago, there dwelt a poor old widow
In a small cottage, by a little meadow
Beside a grove and standing in a dale.
This widow-woman of whom I tell my tale
Since the sad day when last she was a wife
Had led a very patient, simple life.
Little had she in capital or rent,
But still, by making do with what God sent,
She kept herself and her two daughters going.
Three hefty sows – no more – were all her showing,
Three cows as well; there was a sheep called Molly.
Sooty her hall, her kitchen melancholy,
And there she ate full many a slender meal;

Now read the extract opposite, which is taken from the end of the tale.

The cock and the fox

Now when the month in which the world began,
March, the first month, when God created man,
Was over, and the thirty-second day
Thereafter ended, on the third of May
It happened that Chanticleer in all his pride,
His seven wives attendant at his side,
Cast his eyes upward to the blazing sun,
Which in the sign of Taurus then had run
His twenty-one degrees and somewhat more,
And knew by nature and no other lore
That it was nine o'clock. With blissful voice
He crew triumphantly and said, 'Rejoice,
Behold the sun! The sun is up, my seven.
Look, it has climbed forty degrees in heaven,
Forty degrees and one in fact, by this.
Dear Madam Pertelote, my earthly bliss,
Hark to those blissful birds and how they sing!
Look at those pretty flowers, how they spring!
Solace and revel fill my heart!' He laughed.

But in that moment Fate let fly her shaft;
And so it happened as he cast his eye
Towards the cabbage at a butterfly
It fell upon the fox there, lying low.
Gone was all indication then to crow.
'Cok cok,' he cried, giving a sudden start,
As one who feels a terror at his heart,
For natural instinct teaches beasts to flee
The moment they perceive an enemy,
Though they never met with it before.

This Chanticleer was shaken to the core
And would have fled. The fox was quick to say
However, 'Sir! Whither so fast away?
Are you afraid of me, that am your friend?
A fiend, or worse, I should be, to intend
You harm, or practise villainy upon you;
Dear sir, I was not even spying on you!

Truly I came to do no other thing
Than just to lie and listen to you sing.
You have as merry a voice as God has given
To any angel in the courts of Heaven;
To that you add a musical sense as strong
As had Boethius who was skilled in song.
My Lord your Father (God receive his soul!)
Your mother too – how courtly, what control! –
Have honoured my poor house, to my great ease;
And you, sir, too, I should be glad to please.
For, when it comes to singing, I'll say this
(Else may these eyes of mine be barred from bliss),
There never was a singer I would rather
Have heard at dawn than your respected father.
All that he sang came welling from his soul
And how he put his voice under control!
The pains he took to keep his eyes tight shut
In concentration – then the tip-toe strut,
The slender neck stretched out, the delicate beak!
No singer could approach him in technique.'

This Chanticleer began to beat a wing
As one incapable of smelling treason,
So wholly had this flattery ravished reason.
This Chanticleer stood high upon his toes,
He stretched his neck, his eyes began to close,
His beak to open; with his eyes shut tight
He then began to sing with all his might.

Sir Russel Fox leapt in to the attack,
Grabbing his gorge he flung him o'er his back
And off he bore him to the woods, the brute,
And for the moment there was no pursuit.
This blessed widow and her daughters two
Heard all these hens in clamour and halloo
And, rushing to the door at all this shrieking,
They saw the fox towards the covert streaking
And, on his shoulder, Chanticleer stretched flat.
'Look, look!' they cried, 'O mercy, look at that!
Ha! Ha! the fox!' and after him they ran,

27

Animal characters

And stick in hand ran many a serving man,
Ran Coll our dog, ran Talbot, Bran and Shaggy,
And, with a distaff in her hand, ran Maggie,
Ran cow and calf and ran the very hogs
In terror at the barking of the dogs;
The men and women shouted, ran and cursed,
They ran so hard they thought their hearts would burst,
They yelled like fiends in Hell, ducks left the water
Quacking and flapping as on point of slaughter.

And now, good people, pay attention all.
See how Dame Fortune quickly changes side
And robs her enemy of hope and pride!
This cock that lay upon the fox's back
In all his dread contrived to give a quack
And said, 'Sir Fox, if I were you, as God's
My witness, I would round upon these clods
And shout, "Turn back, you saucy bumpkins all!
A very pestilence upon you fall!
Now that I have in safety reached the wood
Do what you like, the cock is mine for good;
I'll eat him there in spite of every one."'
The fox replying, 'Faith, it shall be done!'
Opened his mouth and spoke. The nimble bird,
Breaking away upon the uttered word,
Flew high into the tree-tops on the spot.
And when the fox perceived where he had got,
'Alas,' he cried, 'alas, my Chanticleer,
I've done you grievous wrong, indeed I fear
I must have frightened you; I grabbed too hard
But, sir, I meant no harm, don't be offended,
Come down and I'll explain what I intended;
So help me God I'll tell the truth – on oath!'
'No,' said the cock, 'and curses on us both,
And first on me if I were such a dunce
As let you fool me oftener than once.
Never again, for all your flattering lies,
You'll coax a song to make me blink my eyes;
And as for those who blink when they should look,

God blot them from his everlasting Book!'
'Nay, rather,' said the fox, 'his plagues be flung
On all who chatter that should hold their tongue.'
Lo, such it is not to be on your guard
Against the flatterers of the world, or yard,
And if you think my story is absurd,
A foolish trifle of a beast and bird,
A fable of a fox, a cock, a hen,
Take hold upon the moral, gentlemen.

(*Geoffrey Chaucer*, from *The Nun's Priest's Tale*, translated by *Nevill Coghill*)

Talk about the story in a small group. Answer these questions in your discussion:

- Do you all understand exactly what happened to Chanticleer in the story?
- Were there any sections you did not understand?
- Were there words or phrases and references to other writers and people that confused you?

Share your answers with the rest of the class.

What does the story say about the animals in the barn-yard? What can you say about Chanticleer and the fox?

Write a short description of each character.

2 Write your own fable

Using the fable on page 25 to help you, write *two* fables of your own in the same style as Aesop.

In the first, retell the story of Chanticleer as Aesop might have done.

In the second, make up a fable of your own about an animal in a school setting.

Use these ideas to help you:

- Arriving at school on time
- School dinners
- Preparing for tests
- Getting up in time for school
- Rushing work instead of taking your time.

Anthropomorphism

Anthropomorphism describes what the writers of all the stories in this unit do to make their stories interesting. Anthropomorphism means giving human characteristics, like the ability to talk, to animals or other objects. You will find examples of anthropomorphism in almost any story about animals you read.

Animal characteristics

The natural behaviour of animals and years of storytelling combine to make people think of animals in certain ways. We think owls are wise, cats are independent, and the lion is the king of the beasts. The reality, in fact, is quite different. Birds have tiny brains, cats like familiar people and places and, in a pride of lions, it is the lioness who is in charge.

Animals have different meanings in different cultures. *You* may not like spiders, but in some areas of the world they are seen as wise and a sign of good luck.

In English stories, cunning or bad animals include foxes, stoats, weasels, crows and magpies. Elephants, badgers and owls are wise, geese and cows are stupid, and horses are brave and noble.

See if these characteristics are given to animals in the stories you read.

3 Showing animals as animals

Some writers have tried to write animal stories which also show something of how real animals behave. These stories are not realistic, but they do say something about the animal world, as in this extract from *The Second Jungle Book* by Rudyard Kipling.

How fear came

And the heat went on and on, and sucked up all the moisture, till at last the main channel of the Waingunga was the only stream that carried a trickle of water between its dead banks; and when Hathi, the Wild Elephant, who lives for a hundred years and more, saw a long, lean blue ridge of rock show dry in the very centre of the stream, he knew that he was looking at the Peace Rock, and then and there he lifted up his trunk and proclaimed the Water Truce, as his father before him had proclaimed it fifty years ago. The deer, wild pig, and buffalo took up the cry hoarsely; and Chil, the Kite, flew in great circles far and wide, whistling and shrieking the warning.

By the Law of the Jungle it is death to kill at the drinking-places when once the Water Truce has been declared. The reason of this is that drinking comes before eating. Every one in the Jungle can scramble along somehow when only game is scarce; but water is water, and when there is but one source of supply, all hunting stops while the Jungle-People go there for their needs. In good seasons, when water was plentiful, those who came down to drink at the Waingunga – or anywhere else, for that matter – did so at the risk of their lives, and that risk made no small part of the fascination of the night's doings. To move down so cunningly that never a leaf stirred; to wade knee-deep in the roaring shallows that drown all noise from behind; to drink, looking backward over one shoulder, every muscle ready for the first desperate bound of keen terror; to roll on the sandy margin, and return, wet-muzzled and well plumped out, to the admiring herd, was a thing that all tall-antlered young bucks took a delight in, precisely because they knew that at any moment Bagheera or Shere Khan might leap upon them and bear them down. But now all that life-and-death fun was ended, and the Jungle-People came up, starved and weary, to the shrunken river, – tiger, bear, deer, buffalo, and pig, all together, – drank the fouled waters, and hung above them, too exhausted to move off.

The deer and the pig had tramped all day in search of something better than dried bark and withered leaves. The buffaloes had found no wallows to be cool in, and no green crops to steal. The snakes had left the Jungle and come down to the river in the hope of finding a stray frog. They curled round wet stones, and never offered to strike when the nose of a rooting pig dislodged them. The river-turtles had long ago been killed by Bagheera, cleverest of hunters, and the fish had buried themselves deep in the dry mud. Only the Peace Rock lay across the shallows like a long snake, and the little tired ripples hissed as they dried on its hot side.

It was here that Mowgli came nightly for the cool and the companionship. The most hungry

"THE WATER CANNOT LIVE LONG," SAID BALOO

of his enemies would hardly have cared for the boy then. His naked hide made him seem more lean and wretched than any of his fellows. His hair was bleached to tow colour by the sun; his ribs stood out like the ribs of a basket, and the lumps on his knees and elbows, where he was used to track on all fours, gave his shrunken limbs the look of knotted grass-stems. But his eye, under his matted forelock, was cool and quiet, for Bagheera was his adviser in this time of trouble, and told him to go quietly, hunt slowly, and never, on any account, to lose his temper.

'It is an evil time,' said the Black Panther, one furnace-hot evening, 'but it will go if we can live till the end. Is thy stomach full, Man-cub?'

'There is stuff in my stomach, but I get no good of it. Think you, Bagheera, the Rains have forgotten us and will never come again?'

'Not I! We shall see the *mohwa* in blossom yet, and the little fawns all fat with new grass. Come down to the Peace Rock and hear the news. On my back, Little Brother.'

'This is no time to carry weight. I can still stand alone, but – indeed we be no fatted bullocks, we two.'

Bagheera looked along his ragged, dusty flank and whispered: 'Last night I killed a bullock under the yoke. So low was I brought that I think I should not have dared to spring if he had been loose. *Wou!*'

Mowgli laughed. 'Yes, we be great hunters now,' said he. 'I am very bold – to eat grubs,' and the two came down together through the crackling undergrowth to the river-bank and the lace-work of shoals that ran out from it in every direction.

'The water cannot live long,' said Baloo, joining them. 'Look across. Yonder are trails like the roads of Man.'

On the level plain of the farther bank the stiff jungle-grass had died standing, and, dying, had mummied. The beaten tracks of the deer and the pig, all heading toward the river, had striped that colourless plain with dusty gullies driven through the ten-foot grass, and, early as it was, each long avenue was full of first-comers hastening to the water. You could hear the does and fawns coughing in the snuff-like dust.

Up-stream, at the bend of the sluggish pool round the Peace Rock, and Warden of the Water Truce, stood Hathi, the wild elephant, with his sons, gaunt and grey in the moonlight, rocking to and fro – always rocking. Below him a little were the vanguard of the deer; below these, again, the pig and the wild buffalo; and on the opposite bank, where the tall trees came down to the water's edge, was the place set apart for the Eaters of Flesh – the tiger, the wolves, the panther, the bear, and the others.

'We are under one Law, indeed,' said Bagheera, wading into the water and looking across at the lines of clicking horns and starting eyes where the deer and the pig pushed each other to and fro. 'Good hunting, all you of my blood,' he added, lying down at full length, one flank thrust out of the shallows; and then, between his teeth, 'But for that which is the Law it would be *very* good hunting.'

The quick-spread ears of the deer caught the last sentence, and a frightened whisper ran along the ranks. 'The Truce! Remember the Truce!'

'Peace there, peace!' gurgled Hathi, the wild elephant. 'The Truce holds, Bagheera. This is no time to talk of hunting.'

'Who should know better than I?' Bagheera answered, rolling his yellow eyes up-stream. 'I am an eater of turtles — a fisher of frogs. *Ngaayah!* Would I could get good from chewing branches!'

'We wish so, very greatly,' bleated a young fawn, who had only been born that spring, and did not at all like it. Wretched as the Jungle-People were, even Hathi could not help chuckling; while Mowgli, lying on his elbows in the warm water, laughed aloud, and beat up the scum with his feet.

'Well spoken, little bud-horn,' Bagheera purred. 'When the truce ends that shall be remembered in thy favour,' and he looked keenly through the darkness to make sure of recognising the fawn again.

Gradually the talking spread up and down the drinking-places. One could hear the scuffling, snorting pig asking for more room; the buffaloes grunting among themselves as they lurched out across the sand-bars, and the deer telling pitiful stories of their long foot-sore wanderings in quest of food. Now and again they asked some question of the Eaters of Flesh across the river, but all the news was bad, and the roaring hot wind of the Jungle came and went between the rocks and the rattling branches, and scattered twigs and dust on the water.

'The men-folk, too, they die beside their ploughs,' said a young sambhur. 'I passed three between sunset and night. They lay still, and their Bullocks with them. We also shall lie still in a little.'

'The river has fallen since last night,' said Baloo. 'O Hathi, hast thou ever seen the like of this drought?'

'It will pass, it will pass,' said Hathi, squirting water along his back and sides.

'We have one here that cannot endure long,' said Baloo; and he looked toward the boy he loved.

'I?' said Mowgli indignantly, sitting up in the water. 'I have no long fur to cover my bones, but — but if *thy* hide were taken off, Baloo — '

Hathi shook all over at the idea, and Baloo said severely:

'Man-cub, that is not seemly to tell a Teacher of the Law. *Never* have I been seen without my hide.'

'Nay, I meant no harm, Baloo, but only that thou art, as it were, like the cocoanut in the husk, and I am the same cocoanut all naked. Now that brown husk of thine — ' Mowgli was sitting cross-legged, and explaining things with his forefinger in his usual way, when Bagheera put out a paddy paw and pulled him over backward into the water.

'Worse and worse,' said the Black Panther, as the boy rose sputtering. 'First Baloo is to be skinned, and now he is a cocoanut. Be careful that he does not do what the ripe cocoanuts do.'

Animal characters

'And what is that?' said Mowgli, off his guard for the minute, though that is one of the oldest catches in the Jungle.

'Break thy head,' said Bagheera quietly, pulling him under again.

Rudyard Kipling (from *The Second Jungle Book*)

Write your answers to these questions:

a   What happens in the extract?

b   Which parts of the story did you find interesting? What aspects of the story failed to hold your attention?

c   How do Mowgli and the animals talk? Why do you think they are made to talk in different ways?

d   Which parts of the story are most realistic?

e   Which parts would certainly be described as 'fantasy'?

Did you enjoy reading the extract?

This next extract is taken from *Black Beauty* by Anna Sewell.

A happy ending

I shall never forget my new master; he had black eyes and a hook nose, his mouth was as full of teeth as a bulldog's, and his voice was as harsh as the grinding of cart wheels over gravel stones. His name was Nicholas Skinner, and I believe he was the same man that poor Seedy Sam drove for.

I have heard men say that seeing is believing; but I should say that *feeling* is believing; for much as I had seen before, I never knew till now the utter misery of a cab-horse's life.

Skinner had a low set of cabs and a low set of drivers; he was hard on the men, and the men were hard on the horses. In this place we had no Sunday rest, and it was in the heat of summer.

Sometimes on a Sunday morning, a party of fast men would hire the cab for the day; four of them inside and another with the driver, and I had to take them ten or fifteen miles out into the country, and back again: never would any of them get down to walk up a hill, let it be ever so steep, or the day ever so hot – unless, indeed, when the driver was afraid I could not manage it, and sometimes I was so fevered and worn that I could hardly touch my food. How I used to long for the nice bran mash with nitre in it that Jerry used to give us on Saturday nights in hot weather, that used to cool us down and make us so comfortable. Then we had two nights and a whole day for unbroken rest, and on Monday morning we were as fresh as young horses again;

but here, there was no rest, and my driver was just as hard as his master. He had a cruel whip with something so sharp at the end that it sometimes drew blood, and he would even whip me under the belly, and flip the lash out at my head. Indignities like these took the heart out of me terribly, but still I did my best and never hung back; for, as poor Ginger said, it was no use; men are the strongest.

My life was now so utterly wretched, that I wished I might, like Ginger, drop down dead at work, and be out of my misery; and one day my wish very nearly came to pass.

I went on the stand at eight in the morning, and had done a good share of work, when we had to take a fare to the railway. A long train was just expected in, so my driver pulled up at the back of some of the outside cabs, to take the chance of a return fare. It was a very heavy train, and as all the cabs were soon engaged, ours was called for. There was a party of four; a noisy, blustering man with a lady, a little boy, and a little girl, and a great deal of luggage. The lady and the boy got into the cab, and while the man ordered about the luggage, the young girl came and looked at me.

'Papa,' she said, 'I am sure this poor horse cannot take us and all our luggage so far, he is so weak and worn up. Do look at him.'

'Oh, he's all right, miss,' said my driver. 'He's strong enough.'

The porter, who was pulling about some heavy boxes, suggested to the gentleman, as there was so much luggage, whether he could not take a second cab.

'Can your horse do it, or can't he?' said the blustering man.

'Oh, he can do it all right, sir. Send up the boxes, porter; he could take more than that,' and he helped to haul up a box so heavy that I could feel the springs go down.

'Papa, papa, do take a second cab,' said the young girl in a beseeching tone; 'I am sure we are wrong, I am sure it is very cruel.'

'Nonsense, Grace, get in at once, and don't make all this fuss; a pretty thing it would be if a man of business had to examine every cab-horse before he hired it – the man knows his own business, of course. There, get in and hold your tongue!'

My gentle friend had to obey; and box after box was dragged up and lodged on the top of the cab, or settled by the side of the driver. At last all was ready, and with his usual jerk at the rein, and slash of the whip, he drove out of the station.

The load was very heavy, and I had had neither food nor rest since the morning; but I did my best, as I always had done, in spite of cruelty and injustice.

I got along fairly till we came to Ludgate Hill, but there the heavy load and my own exhaustion were too much. I was struggling to keep on, goaded by constant chucks of the rein and use of the whip, when, in a single moment – I cannot tell how – my feet flipped from under me, and I fell heavily to the ground on my side; the suddenness and the force with which I fell

seemed to beat all the breath out of my body. I lay perfectly still; indeed, I had no power to move, and I thought now I was going to die. I heard a sort of confusion round me, loud angry voices, and the getting down of the luggage, but it was all like a dream. I thought I heard that sweet pitiful voice saying, 'Oh, that poor horse! It is all our fault.' Someone came and loosened the throat strap of my bridle, and undid the traces which kept the collar so tight upon me. Someone said, 'He's dead, he'll never get up again.' Then I could hear a policeman giving orders, but I did not even open my eyes, I could only draw a grasping breath now and then. Some cold water was thrown over my head, and some cordial was poured into my mouth, and something was covered over me. I cannot tell how long I lay there, but I found my life coming back, and a kind-voiced man was patting me and encouraging me to rise. After some more cordial had been given me, and after one or two attempts, I staggered to my feet, and was gently led to some stables close by. Here I was put into a well-littered stall, and some warm gruel was brought to me, which I drank thankfully.

In the evening I was sufficiently recovered to be led back to Skinner's stables, where I think they did the best for me they could. In the morning Skinner came with a farrier to look at me. He examined me very closely, and said:

'This is a case of overwork more than disease, and if you could give him a run off for six months, he would be able to work again; but now there is not an ounce of strength in him.'

'Then he must just go to the dogs,' said Skinner; 'I have no meadows to nurse sick horses in —

he might get well or he might not; that sort of thing don't suit my business, my plan is to work 'em as long as they'll go, and then sell 'em for what they'll fetch, at the knacker's or elsewhere.'

'If he was broken-winded,' said the farrier, 'you had better have him killed out of hand, but he is not. There is a sale of horses coming off in about ten days; if you rest him and feed him up, he may pick up, and you may get more than his skin is worth, at any rate.'

Upon this advice, Skinner, rather unwillingly, I think, gave orders that I should be well fed and cared for, and the stable man, happily for me, carried out the orders with a much better will than his master had in giving them. Ten days of perfect rest, plenty of good oats, hay, bran mashes, with boiled linseed mixed in them, did more to get my condition than anything else could have done; those linseed mashes were delicious, and I began to think, after all, it might be better to live than go to the dogs. When the twelfth day after the accident came, I was taken to the sale, a few miles out of London. I felt that any change from my present place must be an improvement, so I held up my head, and hoped for the best.

Anna Sewell (from Black Beauty)

What does this extract say about animals and people? Think about:

- how the story is told and who tells it

- how the horse's life is described

- how people are described.

4 Making animals real

Some writers have attempted to convey *exactly* what an animal's life is like. Read the extract below from *White Fang* by Jack London. Jack London attempts to write from the point of view of a wolf cub.

The grey cub

He was a fierce little cub. So were his brothers and sisters. It was to be expected. He was a carnivorous animal. He came of a breed of meat-killers and meat-eaters. His father and mother lived wholly upon meat. The milk he had sucked with his first flickering life was milk transformed directly from meat; and now, at a month old, when his eyes had been open for about a week, he was beginning himself to eat meat — meat half digested by the she-wolf and disgorged for the five growing cubs that already made too great demand upon her breast.

But he was, further, the fiercest of the litter. He could make a louder rasping growl than any of them. His tiny rages were much more terrible than theirs. It was he that first learned the trick of rolling a fellow-cub over with a cunning paw-stroke. And it was he that first gripped another cub by the ear and pulled and tugged and growled through jaws tight-clenched. And certainly it was he that caused the mother the most trouble in keeping her litter from the mouth of the cave.

The fascination of the light for the grey cub increased from day to day. He was perpetually departing on yard-long adventures toward the cave's entrance, and as perpetually being driven back. Only he did not know it for an entrance. He did not know anything about entrances — passages whereby one goes from one place to another place. He did not know any other place, much less of a way to get there. So to him the entrance of the cave was a wall — a wall of light. As the sun was to the outside dweller, this wall was to him the sun of his world. It attracted him as a candle attracts a moth. He was always striving to attain it. The life that was so swiftly expanding within him urged him continually toward the wall of light. The life that was within him knew that it was the one way out, the way he was predestined to tread. But he himself did not know anything about it. He did not know there was any outside at all.

There was one strange thing about this wall of light. His father (he had already come to recognise his father as the one other dweller in the world, a creature like his mother, who slept near the light and was a bringer of meat) — his father had a way of walking right into the white far wall and disappearing. The grey cub could not understand this. Though never permitted by his mother to approach that wall, he had approached the other walls, and encountered hard obstruction on the end of his tender nose. This hurt. And after several such adventures, he left the walls alone. Without thinking about it, he accepted this disappearing into the wall as a peculiarity of his father, as milk and half-digested meat were peculiarities of his mother.

In fact, the grey cub was not given to thinking — at least, the kind of thinking customary of men. He had a method of accepting things without questioning the why and wherefore. In reality, this was the act of classification. He was never

disturbed over *why* a thing happened. *How* it happened was sufficient for him. Thus, when he had bumped his nose on the back wall a few times, he accepted that he would not disappear into walls. In the same way he accepted that his father could disappear into walls. But he was not in the least disturbed by desire to find out the reason for the difference between his father and himself. Logic and physics were no part of his mental make-up.

Like most creatures of the Wild, he early experienced famine. There came a time when not only did the meat-supply cease, but the milk no longer came from his mother's breast. At first the cubs whimpered and cried, but for the most part they slept. It was not long before they were reduced to a coma of hunger. There were no more spats and squabbles, no more tiny rages nor attempts at growling; while the adventures toward the far white wall ceased altogether. The cubs slept, while the life that was in them flickered and died down.

One Eye (the cub's father) was desperate. He ranged far and wide, and slept but little in the lair that had now become cheerless and miserable. The she-wolf, too, left her litter and went out in search of meat. In the first days after the birth of the cubs, One Eye had journeyed several times back to the Indian camp and robbed the rabbit snares; but, with the melting of the snow and the opening of the streams, the Indian camp had moved away, and that source of supply was closed to him.

When the grey cub came back to life and again took interest in the far white wall, he found that the population of his world had been reduced.

Only one sister remained to him. The rest were gone. As he grew stronger, he found himself compelled to play alone, for the sister no longer lifted her head nor moved about. His little body rounded out with the meat he now ate; but the food had come too late for her. She slept continuously, a tiny skeleton flung round with skin, while the flame flickered lower and lower and at last went out.

Then there came a time when the grey cub no longer saw his father appearing and disappearing in the wall, nor lying down asleep in the entrance. This had happened at the end of a second and less severe famine. The she-wolf knew why One Eye never came back, but there was no way by which she could tell what she had seen to the grey cub. Hunting herself for meat, up the left fork of the stream where lived the lynx, she had followed a day-old trail of One Eye. And she had found him, or what remained of him, at the end of the trail. There were many signs of the battle that had been fought, and of the lynx's withdrawal to her lair after having won the victory. Before she went away, the she-wolf had found this lair, but the signs told her that the lynx was inside, and she had not dared to venture in.

After that, the she-wolf in her hunting avoided the left fork. For she knew that in the lynx's lair was a litter of kittens, and she knew the lynx for a fierce, bad-tempered creature and a terrible fighter. It was all very well for half a dozen wolves to drive a lynx, spitting and bristling, up a tree; but it was quite a different matter for a lone wolf to encounter a lynx – especially when the lynx was known to have a litter of hungry kittens at her back.

But the Wild is the Wild, and motherhood is motherhood, at all times fiercely protective whether in the Wild or out of it; and the time was to come when the she-wolf, for her grey cub's sake, would venture the left fork, and the lair in the rocks, and the lynx's wrath.

Jack London (from *White Fang*)

How successful has Jack London been in writing from the point of view of a wolf cub?

Write your answers to these questions:

a What do you learn from this extract about the way wolves behave?

b Does the wolf cub or its mother have any human characteristics? What evidence can you find for these?

c How has Jack London tried to make his story interesting to his readers?

Judging by this extract, how successful a story is *White Fang*? Working as a small group, organise a discussion.

Choose a chairperson or interviewer. One person in the group should then pretend to be the writer of the extract, Jack London.

Then, introduced by the interviewer, the writer should explain what he or she was trying to achieve in the story.

5 Writing an animal story

Write a story of your own in which an animal is the central character. Use your story to say something about the attitudes people have towards animals. Before you start to write, think about:

- **Who will tell the story?**
  Will you write the story as if from the outside or will you tell it through an animal's eyes? If you write from an animal's point of view, will the animal be the central character in your story?

- **What kind of characteristics will you give your animal?**
  Will they be what people expect or will they challenge the reader to look at the animal in another way?

- **Will your story have a message?**
  Will the animal's behaviour say something about human actions and qualities?

- **Who is the audience for the story?**
  Are your readers likely to be children? How old will they be?
  Will you have to think about the cruelty of some scenes?

Next ...

- Do some research into the animal you will be writing about; this way, you can include some interesting details that most people will not know.

- Draft your writing carefully. Discuss the drafts with a partner and listen to his or her ideas. Many animal stories benefit from illustration. Think about whether pictures would help your story.

- After a careful revision of your draft, write the final version.

on target?

After working through this unit, could you:

- describe three different ways in which animals are portrayed in books and stories?

- explain what anthropomorphism means?

- discuss the main features of another animal story?

Design and presentation

All writers know that the way their words look on a page is sometimes nearly as important as the words themselves.

 In this unit, you will be talking about presentation and how the shape of a poem can add to its meaning.

1 Thinking about presentation

How important a part does presentation play in the nine items of writing listed below?

> Discuss the list with a partner. Decide in which of these pieces of writing presentation is most important, and in which it is least important.
>
> You could also arrange the items in a shape or form that shows clearly which item is most important and which is least important.
>
> - a job application letter
> - a story for a young child
> - notes taken during a talk by a visiting speaker
> - an exam essay
> - notes for an announcement in assembly
> - an entry in a private diary
> - an advert to sell a second-hand bike
> - notes for a debate speech
> - a letter thanking a relative for a present.
>
> Compare your lists with others. Discuss the reasons for any differences you find.
>
> Decide which pieces of writing would be best presented using a word-processor.

Skills Box

Understanding what a poem looks like

The layout of text in most books *looks* the same. The text starts on the left-hand margin and crosses the page until it reaches the right-hand margin, as this paragraph does. Both these margins form straight lines. This layout is called 'justified'.

The lines of a poem normally start at the left-hand margin – but not always. And, most of the time, there is no fixed right-hand margin, so that the right side of a poem will often have a ragged look. The layout of this paragraph is called 'unjustified'.

What a poem looks like influences the way we read it. Short lines, for example, usually produce a jerky, nervous rhythm. Longer lines lead to a rhythm which flows more and is more relaxed. Look at the poem on the right:

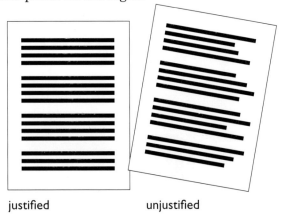

justified   unjustified

Daffodils

I wandered lonely as a cloud
That floats on high o'er vales and hills,
When all at once I saw a crowd,
A host, of golden daffodils;
Beside the lake, beneath the trees,
Fluttering and dancing in the breeze.

Continuous as the stars that shine
And twinkle on the milky way,
They stretched in never-ending line
Along the margin of a bay:
Ten thousand saw I at a glance,
Tossing their heads in sprightly dance.

The waves beside them danced; but they
Out-did the sparkling waves in glee:
A poet could not but be gay,
In such a jocund company:
I gazed — and gazed — but little thought
What wealth the show to me had brought:

For oft, when on my couch I lie
In vacant or in pensive mood,
They flash upon that inward eye
Which is the bliss of solitude;
And then my heart with pleasure fills,
And dances with the daffodils.

William Wordsworth

The way a poem looks also influences how we understand it. Quite often a poet presents a poem in a particular way on the page because that 'look' conveys the meaning of the poem as much as the words themselves.

2 Looking at the form of poetry

Read the poem below. It has been reproduced as if it was a piece of prose.

Breathless
(Written at 21,200 feet on May 23rd)

Heart aches, lungs pant – the dry air sorry, scant. Legs lift and why at all? Loose drift, heavy fall. Prod the snow its easiest way; a flat step is holiday. Look up, the far stone is many miles far and alone. Grind the breath once more and on; don't look up till journey's done. Must look up – glasses are dim. Wrench of hand is breathless limb. Pause one step, breath swings back; swallow once, dry throat is slack. Then on to the far stone; don't look up, count the steps done. One step, one heart-beat, stone no nearer dragging feet. Heart aches, lungs pant – the dry air sorry, scant.

Wilfred Noyce

Discuss this poem with a partner.

How easy did you find it to read?

What do you think the poem is about?

How good a poem do you think this is?

Now read the same poem again. This time, however, it has been reproduced as the poet intended: the poem is printed over the page.

Breathless
(Written at 21,200 feet on May 23rd)

Heart aches,
Lungs pant
The dry air
Sorry, scant.
Legs lift
And why at all?
Loose drift,
Heavy fall.
Prod the snow
Its easiest way;
A flat step
Is holiday.
Look up,
The far stone
Is many miles
Far and alone.
Grind the breath
Once more and on;
Don't look up
Till journey's done.

Must look up
Glasses are dim.
Wrench of hand
Is breathless limb.
Pause one step,
Breath swings back;
Swallow once,
Dry throat is slack.
Then on
To the far stone;
Don't look up,
Count the steps done.
One step,
One heart-beat,
Stone no nearer
Dragging feet.
Heart aches,
Lungs pant
The dry air
Sorry, scant.

Wilfred Noyce

With your partner, discuss the poem again.

How easy did you find it to read the poem like this?

Is it easier to see what the poem is about?

Has your opinion of the poem changed?

46

3 Using presentation in poetry

The poems on these pages all use presentation for effect in startling ways.

```
                          r
                  a           a
              t                   p
            s                       u
  e v e n i n g           n c t u a l
    e                                 g
    h                               e
    T                             m
    s                           m
    h                         e
    i                       d
  n e s   l i k       a h ' s   d i a
              e       j
              a       a
                  r
```

Guillaume Apolinaire

```
              I n
            the  spin
          Of  the  sun
        In  the  spuming
      Cyclone  of  his  wing
    For  I  was  lost  who  am
  Crying at the man drenched throne
In  the  first  fury  of  his  stream
And  the  lightnings  of  adoration
  Back to black silence melt and mourn
    For  I  was  lost  who  have  come
      To  dumbfounding  haven
        And  the  finding  one
          And the  high  noon
            Of  his  wound
              Blinds  my
                Cry.
```

Dylan Thomas

Easter-wings

Lord, who createdst man in wealth and store,
Though foolishly he lost the same,
Decaying more and more,
Till he became
Most poore:
With thee
O let me rise
As larks, harmoniously,
And sing this day thy victories:
Then shall the fall further the flight in me.

My tender age in sorrow did beginne:
And still with sickness and shame
Thou didst so punish sinne,
That I became
Most thinne.
With thee
Let me combine
And feel this day thy victorie:
For, if I imp[1] my wing on thine,
Affliction shall advance the flight in me.

1   imp: to engraft feathers in a damaged wing.

George Herbert

Short story

I

wrote

a

great

story

at

school

today

Mum

It

was

60

c

e

n

t

i

m

e

t

r

e

s

long

David R Morgan

Breakfast

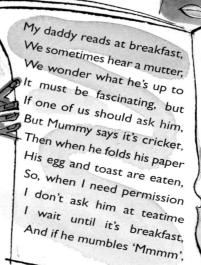

My daddy reads at breakfast,
We sometimes hear a mutter,
We wonder what he's up to
It must be fascinating, but
If one of us should ask him,
But Mummy says it's cricket,
Then when he folds his paper
His egg and toast are eaten,
So, when I need permission
I don't ask him at teatime
I wait until it's breakfast,
And if he mumbles 'Mmmm',
He holds THE TIMES up high.
And sometimes catch a sigh.
Behind that screen of print.
We've not the smallest hint.
He says it's 'world affairs',
Or boring stocks and shares.
And grabs his things to go,
Quite how, we'll never know.
For something I have planned,
— For then he'd understand —
Then make my special plea,
That's good enough for me!

Noel Petty

Friendly warning

LISTEN GRASS, TAKE IT EASY. DON'T GROW TOO TALL. THEY'LL JUST BRING IN A LAWN MOWER AND CUT YOU DOWN SHORT.

SEE? I TOLD YOU THEY WOULD.

Robert Froman

Supermarket

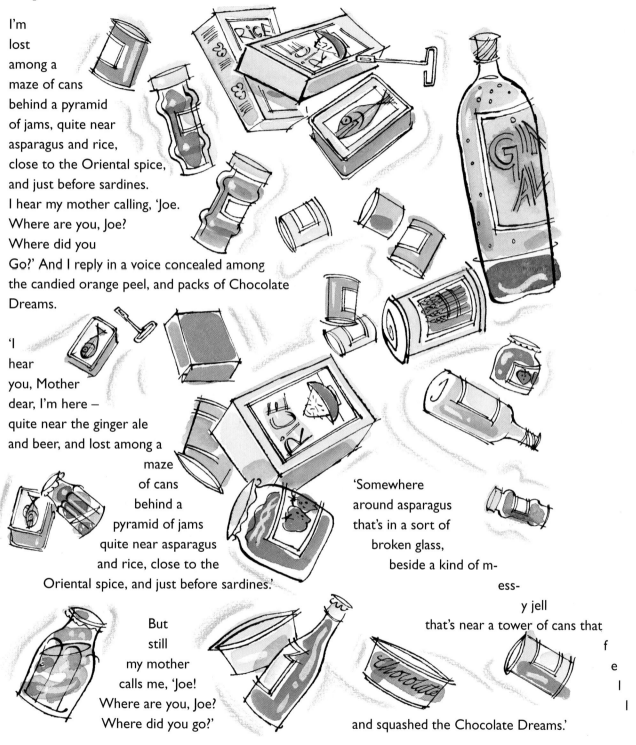

I'm
lost
among a
maze of cans
behind a pyramid
of jams, quite near
asparagus and rice,
close to the Oriental spice,
and just before sardines.
I hear my mother calling, 'Joe.
Where are you, Joe?
Where did you
Go?' And I reply in a voice concealed among
the candied orange peel, and packs of Chocolate
Dreams.

'I
hear
you, Mother
dear, I'm here –
quite near the ginger ale
and beer, and lost among a
maze
of cans
behind a
pyramid of jams
quite near asparagus
and rice, close to the
Oriental spice, and just before sardines.'

But
still
my mother
calls me, 'Joe!
Where are you, Joe?
Where did you go?'

'Somewhere
around asparagus
that's in a sort of
broken glass,
beside a kind of m-

ess-

y jell
that's near a tower of cans that

f
e
l
l

and squashed the Chocolate Dreams.'

Felice Holman

49

Design and presentation

Thank-you letter

Dear Aunty Grace, ~~Mum said I had to~~
I'm writing this letter just to say
~~I hate that terrible dress you sent~~
I adore the dress you sent today.

~~Erk! Mauve!~~ The colour's just terrific!
Those little puff sleeves are really neat!
Frilly socks to match! It's just too much!
~~I'd rather wear blisters on my feet!~~

Mum says the dress looks sweetly charming.
It suits me now I'm growing up.
~~When I was made to try that thing on~~
~~I totally felt like throwing up!~~

The lace around the hem's ~~a nightmare~~
~~I won't wear that ghastly dress!~~ a dream!
I've never seen such pretty ruffles.
~~I hope I wake up before I scream!~~

You shouldn't have spent so much money,
but thanks for such a lovely surprise –
~~of all the dum dum birthday presents,~~
~~yours, Aunty Grace, easily takes first prize!~~

You're very generous. ~~With some luck~~
~~I can lose the socks.~~ So thanks again
~~ink spilled on mauve I hope won't wash out~~
for the wonderful dress! Love from

Robin Klein

Zoo cage

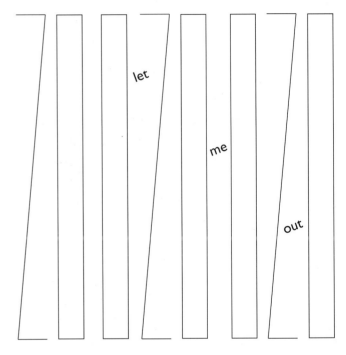

Michael Rosen

For each poem, use a chart like the one below to note down how the poem has been presented. In the third column, say why you think the writer has chosen to present the poem in this way.

Title of poem	How is the poem presented?	Why has the writer done this? What effect is he or she seeking?

Skills Box

Aspects of presentation

Presentation starts with neat handwriting and careful spelling. There are, however, other things that can affect the appearance of your writing. This is particularly true where you are using a word-processor or desktop publisher for your work.

The size of your writing

Writing always has to be legible (easy to read), but varying the *size* of your writing can be very effective. This is particularly true when preparing magazine and newspaper articles, posters or advertisements.

The size of writing is measured in point sizes. The bigger the point size the larger the print.

The red balloon	12pt
gets bigger	16pt
and bigger	18pt
then explodes	22pt
with a whimper	10pt

Upper case or lower case?

Using UPPER CASE (capital letters) can make parts of your writing stand out more boldly.

When you are handwriting, this is the easiest way to create an alternative style to your usual writing. Use upper case for short pieces of texts only – it is harder to read when it covers more than a few lines.

Mum says, 'Why don't you tidy your room?'
Gran says, 'Will you find my glasses?'
Sharon says, 'Why don't you get your haircut?'
Teacher says, 'Where's your homework?'
I say, **'LEAVE ME ALONE!'**

Text effects and different fonts

Word-processors have meant that almost anyone can use italic (*sloped text, like this*) or bold (**darker text, like this**) writing. It is also possible to use many different typefaces or fonts to give individual letters different shapes.

With handwriting, underlining is one way to add a presentational effect to your work. Another is to use illustration or colour to add to your words.

I unrolled the dusty parchment and <u>with difficulty</u> read its faded message:

 The Captain's treasure is on Skull Island. Fifty yards north of Bear Rock

(Skills box continues over the page.)

Skills Box

Margins, white space and columns
Newspapers and magazines have always used different margins (gaps at the sides of each page) and columns (pillars of short lines of text) to produce different effects. Word-processing means that anyone can achieve the same effects.

Wide *margins* create white space (areas where there is no text) on the page and make it easy for the reader's eyes to cross the page.

Columns create shorter line lengths which are also easier for the eye to scan across.

When you are handwriting, and especially if your writing is small, leave a double line between your paragraphs or a slightly wider margin to make your writing easier to read.

Indenting (starting the first line of a new paragraph slightly in from the left-hand margin) is a simple way to create extra white space on your hand-written page.

Positioning text
The poems in this unit use positioning in all kinds of interesting ways, but any writing can be positioned for effect. The most common forms of positioning for writing are: aligned left, centred and aligned right.

This text is aligned left for effect

This text is centred for effect

This text is aligned right for effect

A final note
The important questions to bear in mind when carrying out work of this kind are:

- What am I adding to the message of the writing?
- Am I making the writer's meaning clearer?

3 Presenting your own writing

To have something to present, you must first have something to say! With a partner, read the poem below. The kind of comparison it uses – where something is said to be 'like' or 'the same as' something else – is called a *simile*. ('Wieners' – in the second to last line – are a kind of German sausage.)

Windigo

Hair like burnt moose moss
Head like a meat ball
Eyes like burning red ashes
Nose like a pig nose
Mouth like a flaming red hoop
Lips like red circles
Voice like an angry moose call
Breath like the dump
Teeth like sharpened swords
Ears like potatoes
Neck like a bear's neck
Body like a giant
Heart like all iceberg
Arms like stretchy telephone wires
Hands like bears' claws
Legs like ice tunnels
Feet like wieners
Toes like sliced apples

Sylvia Mark

With your partner, discuss the comparisons that the poem makes. Most of these describe what the creature looks like.

Look through the poem again. Decide whether these comparisons give you an idea about the colour, the size, the shape or the texture of what is being described.

Pick out similes which are *not* about appearance. Do these appeal to your other senses (hearing, smell, taste, touch) or are they describing something less real, more **abstract**?

Use the poem, 'Windigo', as the starting point for a poem of your own about:

● a mythical beast
● an alien encountered in deep space
● an animal found on Earth.

Use similes to describe the creature.

When you produce the final version of your poem, think about:

● how you can use the shape of the poem to reflect the creature's shape
● varying line lengths and shapes for effect
● using different fonts and text effects
● how you want to position your text on the page.

Prepare the final version (word-processed or handwritten) for a class display.

... on using DTP and graphics

If you can import your words into a desktop publisher or graphics program you will find other things you can do with them – enclosing words or phrases in boxes, bending the words or turning them upside-down.

You can achieve the same effects by 'cut and pasting' by hand from your word-processed piece. Doing this and photocopying the results can produce an effective final version. Experiment with ideas that use new technology or blend the old and the new.

Avoid the mistake, which many beginners make, of using too many techniques, too many different sizes and styles.

5 Reviewing your results

As a group, discuss what you have learned about presentation as you review your display.

What does the computer do best? What can pen and paper do that the computer cannot? Does the computer always save time, or are some things more quickly done by hand?

Remember, once you have tried out a range of possibilities, the important thing is to present your poem in the most appropriate way. If you do not, the message you are trying to communicate may be lost.

Decide which of the poems displayed are presented most successfully.

on target

After working through this unit, could you:

- make decisions about whether, and how, to use a computer to improve the appearance of your own writing?

- explain how good presentation of a piece of writing may make its meaning clearer?

- explain how poor presentation may conceal the meaning?

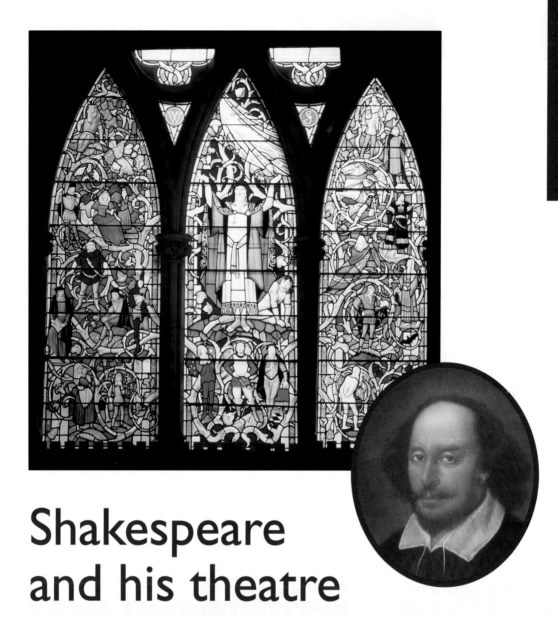

Shakespeare and his theatre

William Shakespeare wrote his plays almost four hundred years ago. What would it have been like to see *Romeo and Juliet* or *Julius Caesar* on the stage at that time? Seeing how the plays might have been performed originally can help you understand them.

◎ **In this unit you will find out about the theatre in Shakespeare's time. You will imagine that you watched one of his plays and see how the stages and actors of his day affected what could be shown on stage.**

55

The theatre in Shakespeare's time

When the young William Shakespeare came from Stratford-upon-Avon to London, new theatre buildings were being built all over the city. There was nothing else like them in the rest of the country. If you wanted to write plays, you went to London, just as film scriptwriters went to Hollywood in the early days of the film industry!

The theatres were built of wood, and none of them is still standing. What we know about them is based on drawings done by people at the time, and on the plans for the Fortune Theatre, which were found long after the building itself had been destroyed. From this evidence, people have attempted to work out just what Shakespeare's theatre, the Globe, looked like.

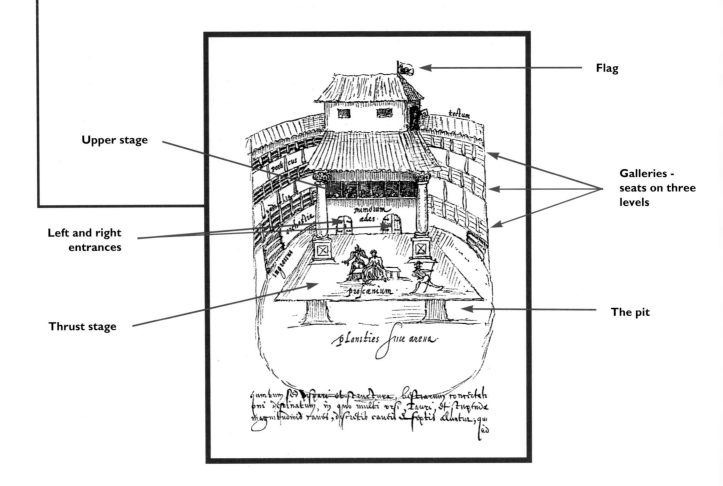

Flag

Galleries - seats on three levels

The pit

Upper stage

Left and right entrances

Thrust stage

Outside

The theatres were round or octagonal (eight-sided). Above the theatre was a flag depicting the theatre's name: a rose, or a swan, or a globe. The flag was raised when the performance was in progress.

Standing room

As you entered the theatre, you would find yourself in an open space rather like a circus ring. This part of the theatre (the pit) was open to the sky. The poorest theatregoers could pay a penny to stand here. Because they stood on the ground, they were called 'groundlings'.

Pies, ale and other food and drink would be sold in the pit, and it would have been crowded and noisy. People in the pit would be there to enjoy the whole experience, not just the play, which it would sometimes be difficult to hear!

Seating

Around the walls of the theatre were three tiers of seats – the galleries. The first gallery was at the same height as the stage, the second gallery at the same height as the upper stage, and the third gallery offered a bird's eye view.

The higher you climbed, the more you paid, and the more exclusive the audience became. Richer people came to the theatre to be seen, as well as to watch the play. Like the groundlings, they enjoyed the social life of the theatre. The round shape of the theatre meant that a large audience could fit into a small space.

The thrust stage

In the middle of the pit, raised just over one and a half metres from the ground, was the stage area. This is where most of the action of the play took place. The stage in the Fortune Theatre measured about 13 x 8 metres: a large space for crowd scenes, and quite a challenge for an actor who had to perform alone, making contact with an audience on three sides of him.

There were no curtains across this stage, so every scene begins with the entrance of actors and ends when they leave. If people 'died' on stage, they had to be carried off. Scenery and large props were carried on and off in full view of the audience.

Entrances and exits

Two trap doors were set into the stage floor. One was called a 'grave trap' and provided a hole actors could stand in. The other was an extra entrance or exit which went right under the stage.

There were two doors at the back of the stage, one on either side: these were the left and right entrance and exit for the actors. Sometimes in Shakespeare's plays, you will see the stage direction 'Exit severally'. At that time 'several' meant 'two', so this meant that both doors would be used.

The inner stage

Between the two doors was a curtain. Some people think this concealed a space that actors used as a dressing room for quick changes. Others think that it may have been a smaller stage, which was used to act out scenes showing private conversations in a small room.

The upper stage

Above the main stage, level with the second gallery, was an upper stage area. This could be used for battlements or to make the actors appear to be far apart.

1 Look at *Julius Caesar* in performance

Julius Caesar was written in 1599 and was one of the first plays staged at the Globe. In the play, a group or Roman senators decide Caesar has become too powerful and that he has ambitions to become a dictator of the Roman Republic. The senators decide he must die.

The tragic hero of the play is Brutus. He has been a good friend of Caesar and only joins the assassins after a lot of persuasion.

Read the extracts from the play that follow. In these scenes, the conspirators make their plans to kill Caesar and carry out the deed.

Extract 1 (Act 1, Scene 2)

CASCA: You pull'd me by the cloak.
Would you speak with me?

BRUTUS: Ay Casca; tell us what hath chanc'd to-day,
That Caesar looks so sad?

CASCA: Why, you were with him, were you not?

BRUTUS: I should not then ask Casca what had chanc'd.

CASCA: Why, there was a crown offer'd him; and being offer'd him, he put it by with the back of his hand, thus; and then the people fell a-shouting.

BRUTUS: What was the second noise for?

CASCA: Why, for that too.

CASSIUS: They shouted thrice; what was the last cry for?

CASCA: Why, for that too.

BRUTUS: Was the crown offer'd him thrice?

CASCA: Ay, marry, was't, and he put it by thrice, every time gentler than other; and at every putting by mine honest neighbours shouted.

CASSIUS: Who offer'd him the crown?

CASCA: Why, Antony.

BRUTUS: Tell us the manner of it, gentle Casca.

CASCA: I can as well be hang'd as tell the manner of it: it was mere foolery; I did not mark it. I saw Mark Antony offer him a crown – yet 'twas not a crown neither 'twas one of these coronets – and, as I told you, he put it by once; but for all that, to my thinking, he would fain have had it. Then he offered it to him again; then he put it by again; but to my thinking, he was very loath to lay his fingers off it. And then he offered it the third time; he put it the third time by; and still as he refus'd it, the rabblement hooted, and clapp'd their chopt hands, and threw up their sweaty night-caps, and uttered such a deal of stinking breath because Caesar refus'd the crown, that it had almost choked Caesar; for he swooned and fell down at it. And for mine own part I durst not laugh, for fear of opening my lips and receiving the bad air.

CASSIUS: But soft, I pray you. What, did Caesar swoon?

CASCA: He fell down in the market-place, and foam'd at mouth, and was speechless.

Extract 2 (Act 3, Scene 1)

Rome. A street before the Capitol.

Flourish. Enter Caesar. Brutus, Cassius, Casca, Decius, Metellus, Trebonius, Cinna, Antony, Lepidus, Artemidorus, Popilius, Publius and the Soothsayer.

CAESAR: The Ides of March are come.

SOOTHSAYER: Ay, Caesar, but not gone.

ARTEMIDORUS: Hail, Caesar! Read this schedule.

DECIUS: Trebonius doth desire you to o'er-read,
At your best leisure, this his humble suit.

ARTEMIDORUS: O Caesar, read mine first; for mine's
[a suit
That touches Caesar nearer. Read it, great
[Caesar.

CAESAR: What touches us ourself shall be last
[serv'd.

ARTEMIDORUS: Delay not, Caesar; read it instantly.

CAESAR: What, is the fellow mad?

PUBLIUS: Sirrah, give place.

CASAR: What, urge you your petitions in the
[street?
Come to the Capitol.

Caesar enters the Capitol, the rest following.

POPILIUS: I wish your enterprise today may thrive.

CASSIUS: What enterprise. Popilius?

POPILIUS: Fare you well.

[Advances to Caesar.]

BRUTUS: What said Popilius Lena?

CASSIUS: He wish'd today our enterprise might
[thrive.
I fear our purpose is discovered.

BRUTUS: Look how he makes to Caesar. Mark him.

CASSIUS: Casca, be sudden, for we fear prevention.

Brutus, what shall be done? If this be known,
Cassius or Caesar never shall turn back,
For I will slay myself.

BRUTUS: Casius, be constant.
Popilius Lena speaks not of our purposes;
For look, he smiles, and Caesar doth not
[change.

CASSIUS: Trebonius knows his time; for look you,
[Brutus,
He draws Mark Antony out of the way.

[Exeunt Antony and Trebonius.]

DECIUS: Where is Metellus Cimber? Let him go
And presently prefer his suit to Caesar.

BRUTUS: He is address'd; press near and second
[him.

CINNA: Casca, you are the first that rears your
[hand.

CAESAR: Are we all ready? What is now amiss
That Caesar and his Senate must redress?

METELLUS: Most high, most mighty, and most
[puissant Caesar,
Metellus Cimber throws before thy seat
An humble heart.

[*Kneeling.*]

CAESAR: I must prevent thee, Cimber.
These couchings and these lowly courtesies
Might fire the blood of ordinary men,
And turn pre-ordinance and first decree
Into the law of children. Be not fond
To think that Caesar bears such rebel blood
That will be thaw'd from the true quality
With that which melteth fools – I mean,
[sweet words,
Low-crooked curtsies, and base spaniel fawning.
Thy brother by decree is banished;
If thou dost bend, and pray, and fawn for him,
I spurn thee like a cur out of my way.
Know, Caesar doth not wrong; not without
[cause
Will he be satisfied.

METELLUS: Is there no voice more worthy than my
[own
To sound more sweetly in great Caesar's ear
For the repealing of my banish'd brother?

BRUTUS: I kiss thy hand, but not in flattery, Caesar,
Desiring thee that Publius Cimber may
Have an immediate freedom of repeal.

CAESAR: What, Brutus!

CASSISUS: Pardon, Caesar! Caesar,
[pardon!
As low as to thy foot doth Cassius fall,
To beg enfranchisement for Publius Cimber.

CAESAR: I could be well mov'd, if I were as you;

If I could pray to move, prayers would move
[me;
But I am constant as the northern star,
Of whose true-fix'd and resting quality
There is no fellow in the firmament.
The skies are painted with unnumb'red
[sparks,
They are all fire, and every one doth shine;
But there's but one in all doth hold his place.
So in the world: 'tis furnish'd well with men,
And men are flesh and blood, and
[apprehensive;
Yet in the number I do know but one
That unassailable holds on his rank,
Unshak'd of motion; and that I am he,
Let me a little show it, even in this –
That I was constant Cimber should be
[banish'd
And constant do remain to keep him so.

CINNA: O Caesar!

CAESAR: Hence! Wilt thou lift up
[Olympus?

DECIUS: Great Caesar!

CAESAR: Doth not Brutus bootless
[kneel?

CASCA: Speak, hands, for me!

[*They stab Caesar. Casca strikes the first, Brutus the last blow.*]

CAESAR: Et tu, Brute? – then fall, Caesar!

William Shakespeare (from *Julius Caesar*)

With a partner, decide how you would present each scene on the stage at the Globe Theatre.

Say how you would use the three stages, the entrances and the trap. Where on the main thrust stage would the actors be at different times?

To help you, note down your answers to these questions:

Extract 1

a   At the start of the extract, Casca is part of Caesar's train. How will Brutus and Cassius manage to attract his attention without making Caesar suspicious?

b   Where should Casca be when he is describing how Caesar was offered the crown?

Extract 2

a   How can you show Caesar surrounded by other characters and still allow the conspirators to talk together?

b   How can you show the conspirators closing in on Caesar, and the murder?

c   What might you do with the body?

3 Look at the setting for *A Midsummer Night's Dream*

Read the extract from *A Midsummer Night's Dream*, on the opposite page.

King Oberon (the Fairy King) has a magic potion. If this potion is rubbed on someone's eyes, that person will fall in love with the first living thing he or she sees on waking up. Oberon finds two uses for this potion: first, to get revenge on his wife, Titania (the Fairy Queen), with whom he has had an argument; secondly, to do a good turn for Helena, one of four young lovers in the play.

The other three young lovers are Lysander, Hermia and Demetrius. Lysander and Hermia are madly in love, but Hermia's father wants her to marry Demetrius, who is also in love with her. Lysander and Hermia have run away. Helena loves Demetrius and has told him of the runaways' plan. Demetrius has followed them, and Helena has followed him. Demetrius cannot stand Helena and tries to lose her in the wood!

Oberon has taken pity on Hermia, after seeing how Demetrius has ill-treated her. He sends his servant, Puck, to look for Demetrius.

From Act 2, Scene 1

[*Enter Puck. He sees Lysander and Hermia asleep
on the ground*]

PUCK: Through the forest have I gone,
But Athenian found I none
On whose eyes I might approve
This flower's force in stirring love.
Night and silence – Who is here?
Weeds of Athens he doth wear:
This is he, my master said,
Despised the Athenian maid:
And here the maiden, sleeping sound,
On the dank and dirty ground.
Pretty soul! she durst not lie
Near this lack-love, this kill-courtesy.
Churl, upon thy eyes I throw
All the power this charm doth owe:
When thou wak'st let love forbid
Sleep his seat on thy eyelid.
So awake when I am gone;
For I must now to Oberon.

[*Exit.*]

[*Enter Demetrius and Helena, running.*]

HELENA: Stay, though thou kill me, sweet
[Demetrius.

DEMETRIUS: I charge thee, hence, and do not haunt
[me thus.

HELENA: O, wilt thou darkling leave me? Do not so.

DEMETRIUS: Stay on thy peril; I alone will go.

[*Exit Demetrius.*]

HELENA: O, I am out of breath in this fond chase!
The more my prayer, the lesser is my grace.
Happy is Hermia, wheresoe'er she lies,
For she hath blessed and attractive eyes.
How came her eyes so bright? Not with salt
[tears:
If so, my eyes are oft'ner washed than hers.
No, no, I am as ugly as a bear;
For beasts that meet me run away for fear.
Therefore no marvel though Demetrius
Do, as a monster, fly my presence thus.
What wicked and dissembling glass of mine
Made me compare with Hermia's sphery eyne?
But who is here? Lysander! on the ground!
Dead, or asleep? I see no blood, no wound.
Lysander, if you live, good sir, awake!

LYSANDER: (*waking*) And run through fire I will for
[thy sweet sake!
Transparent Helena! Nature shows art,
That through thy bosom makes me see thy
[heart.
Where is Demetrius? O, how fit a word
Is that vile name, to perish on my sword!

HELENA: Do not say so, Lysander; say not so:
What though he love your Hermia? Lord,
[what though?
Yet Hermia still loves you; then be content.

LYSANDER: Content with Hermia? No, I do repent
The tedious minutes I with her have spent.
Not Hermia but Helena I love:
Who will not change a raven for a dove?
The will of man is by his reason swayed;
And reason says you are the worthier maid.
Things growing are not ripe until their season;
So I, being young, till now ripe not to reason;
And touching now the point of human skill,
Reason becomes the marshall to my will,
And leads me to your eyes, where I o'erlook
Love's stories, written in love's richest book.

HELENA: Wherefore was I to this keen mockery
[born?
When at your hands did I deserve this scorn?
Is't not enough, is't not enough, young man,
That I did never, no, nor never can
Deserve a sweet look from Demetrius' eye,
But you must flout my insufficiency?
Good troth, you do me wrong, good sooth,
[you do,
In such disdainful manner me to woo.
But fare you well; perforce I must confess

I thought you lord of more true gentleness.
O, that a lady of one man refused
Should of another therefore be abused!

[*Exit.*]

William Shakespeare (from *A Midsummer Night's Dream*)

Make a copy of the diagram of a stage.

Select one particular moment in this scene. Using pieces of card or counters for each character, decide what you think are the positions of all the characters on stage at that moment.

Discuss your decisions with the group.

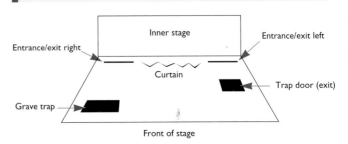

Remember that you can position the characters on the upper stage as well

4 Look at the duel scene in *Romeo and Juliet*

There is an element of bad luck in the story of *Romeo and Juliet*. The hatred between Romeo's family, the Montagues, and Juliet's family, the Capulets, has gone on for generations, so Romeo and Juliet should never have met at all. At the end of the play, after a series of disasters and tragic confusions, Romeo and Juliet both die. The duel is typical of these events.

In the extract below, Romeo's cousin Mercutio and his friend, Benvolio, meet Tybalt Capulet and his friends. An argument starts.

Act 2, Scene 6

[*Enter Tybalt and others.*]

BENVOLIO: By my head, here comes the Capulets!

MERCUTIO: By my heel, I care note.

TYBALT: Follow me close, for I will speak to them.
  Gentlemen, good den; a word with one of
    [you.

MERCUTIO: And but one word with one of us?
  Couple it with something: make it a word and
    [a blow.

TYBALT: You shall find me apt enough to that, sir,
  an you will give me occasion.

MERCUTIO: Could you not take some occasion
  without giving?

TYBALT: Mercutio, thou consortest with Romeo —

MERCUTIO: Consort? What, dost thou make us
  minstrels? An thou make minstrels of us, look
  to hear nothing but discord. Here's my
  fiddlestick; here's that shall make you dance.
  Zounds, consort!

BENVOLIO: We talk here in the public haunt of
    [men.
  Either withdraw unto some private place,
  Or reason coldly of your grievances,
  Or elso depart. Here, all eyes gaze on us.

MERCUTIO: Men's eyes were made to look, and let
    [them gaze;
  I will not budge for no man's pleasure, I.

[*Enter Romeo.*]

TYBALT: Well, peace be with you, sir. Here comes
    [my man.

MERCUTIO: But I'll be hanged, sir, if he wear your
    [livery.
  Marry, go before to field, he'll be your
    [follower:
  Your worship in that sense may call him
    ['man'.

TYBALT: Romeo, the love I bear thee can afford
  No better term than this: thou art a villain.

ROMEO: Tybalt, the reason that I have to love thee
  Doth much excuse the appertaining rage
  To such a greeting. Villain am I none;
  Therefore, farewell; I see thou knowest me
    [not.

TYBALT: Boy, this shall not excuse the injuries
  That thou hast done me; therefore turn and
    [draw.

ROMEO: I do protest I never injured thee,
But love thee better than thou can'st devise
Till thou shalt know the reason of my love;
And so, good Capulet – which name I tender
As dearly as mine own – be satisfied.

MERCUTIO: O calm, dishonourable, vile
[submission!
Alla stoccata carries it away. [*He draws his
sword.*]
Tybalt, you rat-catcher, will you walk?

TYBALT: What would'st thou have with me?

MERCUTIO: Good King of Cats, nothing but one of
your nine lives; that I mean to make bold
withal, and, as you shall use me hereafter,
dry-beat the rest of the eight. Will you pluck
your sword out of his pilcher by the ears?
Make haste, lest mine be about your ears ere
it be out.

TYBALT: (*drawing his sword*) I am for you.

ROMEO: Gentle Mercutio, put thy rapier up.

MERCUTIO: (*to Tybalt*) Come, sir, your passado.

[*Mercutio and Tybalt fight.*]

ROMEO: Draw, Benvolio; beat down their
[weapons.
Gentlemen, for shame, forbear this outrage!
Tybalt! Mercutio! the Prince expressly hath
Forbid this bandying in Verona streets.
Hold, Tybalt! good Mercutio!

[*Romeo comes between them. Tybalt wounds
Mercutio from behind Romeo, then runs away,
followed by his men.*]

MERCUTIO: I am hurt.
A plague a both your houses! I am sped.

Is he gone, and hath nothing?

BENVOLIO: What, art thou hurt?

MERCUTIO: Ay, ay, a scratch, a scratch; marry, 'tis
[enough.
Where is my page? Go, villain, fetch a
[surgeon.

[*Exit Page.*]

ROMEO: Courage, man; the hurt cannot be much.

MERCUTIO: No, 'tis not so deep as a well, nor so
wide as a church door, but 'tis enough, 'twill
serve. Ask for me to-morrow, and you shall
find me a grave man. I am peppered, I
warrant, for this world. A plague a both your
houses! Zounds! a dog, a rat, a mouse, a cat,
to scratch a man to death! A braggart, a
rogue, a villain, that fights by the book of
arithmetic! Why the devil came you between
us? I was hurt under your arm.

ROMEO: I thought all for the best.

MERCUTIO: Help me into some house, Benvolio,
Or I shall faint. A plague a both your houses!
They have made worms' meat of me.
I have it, and soundly too – Your houses!

[*Benvolio helps him out.*]

ROMEO: This gentleman, the Prince's near ally,
My very friend, hath got this mortal hurt
In my behalf; my reputation stained
With Tybalt's slander – Tybalt that an hour
Hath been my cousin. O sweet Juliet,
Thy beauty hath made me effeminate,
And in my temper softened valour's steel.

[*Benvolio returns.*]

BENVOLIO: O Romeo, Romeo, brave Mercutio is
[dead.
That gallant spirit hath aspired the clouds,
Which too untimely here did scorn the earth.

ROMEO: This day's black fate on more days doth
[depend;
This but begins the woe others must end.

[*Tybalt returns.*]

BENVOLIO: Here comes the furious Tyablt back again.

ROMEO: Alive, in triumph! and Mercutio slain!
Away to heaven, respective lenity,
And fire-eyed fury be my conduct now!
Now, Tybalt, take the 'villain' back again
That late thou gavest me, for Mercutio's soul
Is but a little way above our heads,
Staying for thine to keep him company.
Either thou or I, or both, must go with him.

TYBALT: Thou, wretched boy, that did consort
[him here,
Shalt with him hence.

ROMEO: (*drawing his sword*) This shall determine
that.

[*They fight, and Romeo kills Tybalt.*]

BENVOLIO: Romeo, away, be gone!
The citizens are up, and Tybalt slain.
Stand not amazed: the Prince will doom thee
[death
If thou art taken. Hence, be gone, away!

ROMEO: O, I am fortune's fool.

BENVOLIO: Why dost thou stay?

[*Exit Romeo.*]

William Shakespeare (from Romeo and Juliet)

Imagine that you are producing this play on the stage of the Fortune Theatre.

Describe how you would use the entrances and exits and the space of the stage to show the movement and chaos of this scene. Use a diagram to help you.

You will need to think about how:

- the two groups of young men meet
- Romeo tries to avoid the fight
- Mercutio restarts it
- Mercutio gets hurt
- Mercutio's injury and death are shown
- Romeo savagely attacks Tybalt
- to end the scene.

5 Perform a scene from a Shakespeare play

In a group, take one of the extracts you have looked at in this unit and prepare it for performance to the rest of the class.

You will need to think about all the points you have considered already. However, the 'stage' you are to perform on may be smaller than the one you had imagined, and you may not have the costumes and props that you would like. You may, therefore, need to adapt some of the decisions you have made to suit what is available to you.

Think also about your audience. Do you want them to experience the play as it may have been performed in Shakespeare's day? Or would it be more effective if you performed it in a modern setting?

6 Write as one of the audience at the Globe

Imagine you are a member of the public at the Globe about to watch a performance of one of the plays you have read. Describe your visit to the theatre in detail. (Remember that performances took place in the daytime in Shakespeare's time.)

Before you write, think about these questions:

- Who are you? Are you rich or poor? Are you going to the theatre to work, or to enjoy yourself? Are you walking there, or travelling by sedan chair?
- What do you see as you approach the theatre? The building? The surroundings? People in the crowd?
- What do you see once you get inside?
- What is the play like? What can you see? What can you hear?
- What are your thoughts as you go home after the play?

on target

After working through this unit, could you:

- talk about the main features of a theatre in Shakespeare's day?
- talk about how other scenes from Shakespeare's plays were staged?
- write about how the most exciting events in other plays you study might appear on stage?

The Harry Hastings method

Some of the most popular novels, television series and films are concerned with crime. Often, books are *adapted* as films and successful films are published in book form.

In this unit you will read and discuss a crime story. You will be looking closely at the way the story was structured by the writer to make you, the reader, respond to it. Then, you will be using some of the same skills in viewing the story from a new angle.

Getting into the story

The story which follows, *The Harry Hastings Method* by Warner Law, tells of ways to beat a burglar.

> Read the first part of the story together in groups of three.
>
> One of you should read the parts written by the narrator, one the letters from the burglar and the other the letters to the burglar from Harry Hastings.
>
> After your reading of the story, you will be asked to work out what the ending might be.

The Harry Hastings method

Susie Plimson says I should keep on practising my writing. She's been my teacher at Hollywood High Adult Education in the professional writing course and says I am still having trouble with my syntaxes and my tenses, and very kindly gave me private lessons at her place, and she is dark-haired and very pretty and about my age (which is twenty-five).

Susie says if I really want to be a professional writer, I should write about what I really know about — if it is interesting — and while I did do a hitch in the navy some time back, I was on a destroyer tender and never heard a shot fired except in practice, which I don't think is a highly interesting matter to describe.

But one thing I know a lot about is working the houses in the Hollywood hills. The people who live up there are not particularly stinking rich, but then, I've never been interested in valuable paintings or diamond necklaces, anyway, because what do you do with them?

But there are usually portable radios and TV sets and auto tape decks and now and then there is some cash lying around, or a fur, or a few pieces of fairly good jewellery, or maybe a new leather jacket — all things easy to dispose of.

This is an area of winding streets and a lot of trees and bushes, and the houses are mostly set back from the street and are some distance from their neighbours, and so it is an easy vicinity to work.

There's no bus service up there at all, so everybody needs a car or two, and if there is no auto in the carport, you can be pretty sure that no one is home.

There are rural-type mailboxes on the street, and people are always stuffing them with business cards and circulars, like ads for house cleaning and landscaping and such.

So I had a lot of cards printed for various things, like for a house-painting firm, and some for the 'Bulldog Burglar Protection Agency', which say we will install all kinds of silent burglar alarms, and bells will ring in our office and we will have radio cars there in a few minutes.

I also have some Pest Control and House Repair cards. None of these firms exists, of course, but neither do the phone numbers on my cards.

But while I drive slowly around the hills in my little VW bus and put my cards in the boxes, I can get a pretty good idea of who is home and who isn't, and who is gone all day, and so forth.

By the way, my truck is lettered with: H. STRUSSMAN INC. GENERAL HOUSE REPAIRS on one side and FERGUSON PEST CONTROL, EVERYBODY LOVES US BUT YOUR PESTS! on the other side.

I make these up myself. My theory is that nobody can ever see both sides of my truck at the same time, which will really confuse witnesses, if there are any. Of course, I change the truck signs every week, and every month I paint the truck a different colour.

When I decide that a certain house is ripe for hitting, I go up and ring the doorbell. If I am wrong and someone is home — this is seldom — I ask them if their house happens to be

swarming with disease-infested rats. Since there are no rats at all in these hills, they always say no and I leave.

If nobody answers the doorbell, it is, of course, another matter. Most of these houses have locks that could be opened by blindfolded monkeys. Not one of them has any kind of burglar alarm.

There are watchdogs in some houses, but these I avoid, because you never know a friendly dog from a vicious one until you've been chewed up. And, of course, I would not hurt any dog if you paid me.

What I am getting to is about one particular house up there. It's a fairly new one-storey modern style, up a driveway, but you can see the carport from the street below. In casing the place for some time, I figured that a man probably lived there alone.

There was only one car, a great big new Mercedes, and this man drove off every weekday morning at nine. I saw him a few times and he was a nice-looking gentleman of about forty-five. He was always gone all day, so I guessed he had an office job.

So one day, I drove my truck up the driveway and got out and saw a sign: BEWARE OF THE DOG — and, at the same time, this little pooch comes out of a dog door and up to me, and he is a black bundle of hair and the wiggliest, happiest little puppy you ever saw.

I picked him up and let him lick my face and saw that he had a tag on his collar that read: CUDDLES, MY OWNER IS HARRY HASTINGS. There was also a phone number.

I rang the doorbell, but nobody came. The front-door lock was so stupid that I opened it with a plastic card.

Inside — well, you have never seen such a sloppy-kept house. Not dirty — just sloppy. There was five day's worth of dishes in the sink.

I found out later that Harry Hastings has a maid who comes and cleans once a week but, meantime, this character just throws his dirty shirts and socks on the floor. What a slob.

I turned out to be right about his living alone. There was only one single bed in use — which, of course, was not made, and I doubt if he makes it from one year to the next. There was no sign of any female presence, which I don't wonder, the way this Hastings lives.

The Harry Hastings method

One of his rooms is an office, and this was *really* a mess. Papers all over the desk and also all over the floor. This room stank of old cigarette butts, of which smell I am very conscious since I gave up smoking.

From what I found on his desk, I learned that this Harry Hastings is a TV writer. He writes kind of spooky stuff, like this Rodney Serling. I took one of his scripts, to study.

From his income-tax returns, which were lying around for all the world to see, I saw he made nearly $93,000 gross the year before.

But most of the furniture in the house is pretty grubby, and the drapes need replacing, which made me wonder what this character spent all his money on, besides the Mercedes.

He had a new electric typewriter and a great big colour TV set, which would take four men to move, and a hi-fi, but no art objects or decent silver or gold cufflinks or things like that.

It wasn't till I went through his clothes closet that I found out that most of his bread went into his wardrobe. There was about $15000 worth of new apparel in there, most of it hand-tailored and from places like where Sinatra and Dean Martin get their outfits. Very mod and up-to-date.

I tried on a couple of jackets, and it turns out that this Hastings and me are exactly the same size! I mean *exactly*. These clothes looked like they had been tailored for me alone, after six fittings. Only his shoes didn't fit me, sad to say.

I was very pleased, indeed, I can tell you, as I have always had trouble getting fitted off the rack. Also, I like to dress in the latest fashion when I take Susie to nice places.

So I took the entire wardrobe, including shirts and ties. I decided to take the typewriter, which I needed for my writing-class homework. The machine I had kept skipping.

But I wanted to try out the typewriter before I took it, and also I thought I would leave a note for this Hastings, so he wouldn't think I was some kind of crude thug.

So I typed:

> *Dear Mr Hastings,*
>
> *I am typing this to see if your typewriter works OK. I see that it does. I am not taking it to sell but I need it because I am trying to become a professional writer like you, which I know because I saw your scripts on your desk, and I am taking one to help me with my work for studying.*
>
> *I wish to make you a compliment anent your fine wardrobe of clothes. As it happened, they are like they have been made for me only. I am not taking them to sell them but because I need some good clothes to wear. Your shoes do not fit me, so I am leaving them.*
>
> *I am also not taking your hi-fi because there is a terrible screech in the treble. I like your dog, and I will give him a biskit.*
>
> *A Friend*

Well, some three months or so now passed, because there was no sense in hitting Hastings's house again until he had time to get a new bunch of clothes together.

But then I thought the time was ripe. I drove by there again and saw a little VW in the carport, and also, there was a big blonde woman shaking rugs.

I drove up and asked her if her house was swarming with disease-infested rats and she said she didn't think so but that she was only the once-a-week cleaning lady. She sounded Scandinavian. I took note that this was a Wednesday.

I went back the next Monday. No car in the carport. But on the way to the house, there was a new sign, hand-lettered on a board, and it read: BEWARE! VICIOUS WATCHDOG ON DUTY! THIS DOG HAS BEEN TRAINED TO ATTACK AND MEAN IT! YOU HAVE BEEN WARNED! PROCEED NO FARTHER!

Well, this gives me pause, as you can well imagine. But then I remember that this Hastings is a writer with an ingenious and inventive mind, and I do not believe this sign for one moment. Cuddles is my friend.

So I start for the house, and, suddenly, this enormous alsatian jumps through the dog door and runs straight at me, growling and snarling, and then he leaps and knocks me down and, sure enough, starts chewing me to pieces.

But then out comes Cuddles, and I am sure there is a dog language, for he woofed at this monster dog as if in reproach, as if to say, 'Knock it off. This is a friend. Leave him alone.' So pretty soon, both dogs are licking me.

But when I get to the front door, I find that this Hastings has installed a new burglar-proof lock. I walk around the house and find that there are new locks on both the kitchen door and the laundry-room. They must have set Hastings back about 150 bucks.

There are also a lot of sliding-glass doors around the house, but I don't like to break plate glass, because I know how expensive it is to replace.

But I finally locate a little louvred window by the laundry-room door, and I find that by breaking only one louvre and cutting the screen, I can reach through and around and open the door.

Inside, I find that the house is just as messy as before. This guy will *die* a slob.

But when I get to his bedroom, here is this note, taped to his closet door. It is dusty and looks like it has been there for months. It says:

Dear Burglar,

Just in case you are the same young man who was in here a few months ago, I think I must tell you that you have a long way to go before you will be a professional writer.

'Anent' is archaic and should be avoided. A 'wardrobe of clothes' is redundant. It is 'biscuit' not 'biskit'. Use your dictionary!

I know you are a young man, because both my cleaning woman and a nineteen-year-old neighbour have seen you and your truck. If you have gotten this far in my house, you cannot be stupid. Have you ever thought of devoting your talents to something a little higher than burgling people such as me?

Harry Hastings

Inside his closet are two fabulous new suits, plus a really great red-and-blue-plaid cashmere sports coat. I take these and am about to leave when I remember there is something I want to tell Hastings.

In his office, there is a new electric typewriter, on which I type:

Dear Mr Hastings:

Thank you for your help. In return,
I want to tell you that I read the script of yours I took and I think it is pretty good, except that I don't believe that the man should go back to his wife. I mean, after she tried to poison him three times. This is just my opinion, of course.

I do not have a dictionary, so I am taking yours.
Thank you.

A Friend

I, of course, do not take this new typewriter, partly because I already have one and also because I figure he will need it to make money with so he can replace his wardrobe again.

Four months go by before I figure it is time to hit the house again. By this time, my clothes are getting kind of tired, and also the styles have changed some.

This time, when I drive up to the house one afternoon, there is a new hand-lettered sign: THIS HOUSE IS PROTECTED BY THE BULLDOG BURGLAR PROTECTION AGENCY! THERE ARE SILENT ALARMS EVERYWHERE! IF THEY ARE TRIPPED, RADIO CARS WILL CONVERGE AT ONCE! PROCEED NO FURTHER! YOU HAVE BEEN WARNED!

Come *on* now! I and I alone am the *non-existent* Bulldog Burglar Protection Agency! I'd put my card in his mailbox! This is really one cheap stinker, this Harry Hastings.

When I get near the house, the dogs come out, and I give them a little loving, and then I see a note on the front door:

Dear Jack,
Welcome! Hope you had a nice trip. The key is hidden where it always has been. I didn't have to go to work today. I've run down the hill to get some scotch and some steaks. Be back in a few minutes. The gals are coming at six.
Harry

Well, this gives me pause. I finally decide that this is not the right day to hit the house. This could, of course, be another of Hastings's tricks, but I can't be sure. So I leave.

But a few days later, I come back and this same note to Jack is still on the door, only now it is all yellowed. You would think that this lame-brain would at least write a new note every day, welcoming Bert or Sam or Harriet or Hazel or whoever.

The truth is that this Hastings is so damn smart, when you think about it, that he is actually stupid.

The broken louvre and the screen have by now been replaced, but when I break the glass and cut the screen and reach around to open the laundry door, I find that he has installed chains and bolts on the inside.

Well, as any idiot knows, you can't bolt all your doors from the inside when you go out, so one door has to be openable, and I figure it has to be the front door; but the only way I can get in is to break a big frosted-plate-glass window to the left of it and reach through and open the door.

As I said, I'm not happy to break plate glass, but this Hastings has left me no choice, so I knock out a hole just big enough for me to reach through and open the door and go in.

This time, there is *another* note on his closed door.

Dear Burglar,

Are you incapable of pity? By now, you must be the best-dressed burglar in Hollywood. But how many clothes can you _wear_? You might like to know that my burglary insurance has been cancelled. My new watchdog cost me three hundred dollars and I have spent a small fortune on new locks and bolts and chains.

Now I fear you are going to start smashing my plate-glass windows, which can cost as much as two hundred dollars to replace. There is only one new suit in this closet. All my other clothes I keep now either in my car or at my office. Take the suit, if you must, but never return, or you will be sorry, indeed, if you do. I have a terrible revenge in mind.

Harry Hastings

PS You still have time to reform yourself.

PPS I don't like his going back to his poisoning wife, either. But the network insisted on a 'Happy Ending'.

HH

Well, I am not about to fall for all this noise about pity. Any man who has a dog trained to go for me and who uses my own Bulldog Agency against me is not, in my mind, deserving of too much sympathy.

So I take the suit, which is a just beautiful Edwardian eight-button, in grey shark-skin.

Now, quite a few months pass and I begin to feel

a little sorry for this character, and I decide to let him alone, forever.

But then, one day, when I am out working, some louse breaks into my own pad, which is three rooms over a private garage in Hollywood. He takes every stitch of clothing I own.

By this time, I am heavily dating Susie Plimson, and she likes good dressers. So, while I am not too happy about it, I decide I have to pay Hastings another visit.

No dogs come out this time when I walk to the front door. But on it is a typed note, which says:

> HELGA! DO NOT OPEN THIS DOOR! Since you were here last week, I bought a PUMA for burglar protection. This is a huge cat, a cougar or a mountain lion, about four feet long, not including the tail. The man I bought it from told me it was fairly tame, but it is *NOT*!
>
> It has tried to attack both dogs, who are OK and are locked in the guest room. I myself have just gone down to my doctor's to have stitches taken in my face and neck and arms. This ferocious puma is wandering loose inside the house.
>
> The SPCA people are coming soon to capture it and take it away. I tried to call you and tell you not to come today, but you had already left. Whatever you do, if the SPCA has not come before you, DO NOT UNDER ANY CIRCUMSTANCES OPEN THIS DOOR!!

Well naturally, this gave me considerable pause. Helga was obviously the blonde cleaning woman. But this was a Tuesday, and she came on Wednesdays. Or she used to. But she could have changed her days.

I stroll around the outside of the house. But all of the curtains and drapes are drawn, and I can't see in. As I pass the guest-room windows, the two dogs bark inside. So this much of the note on the door is true.

So I wander back to the front door, and I think and I ponder. Is there really a puma in there, or is this just another of Hastings's big fat dirty lies?

After all, it is one hell of a lot of trouble to buy and keep a puma just to protect a few clothes. And it is also expensive, and this Hastings I know by now is a cheapskate.

It costs him not one thin dime to put this stupid note to Helga on his front door and, God knows, it would terrify most anybody who wanted to walk in.

Susie told us in class that, in every story, there is like a moment of decision. I figured this was mine.

After about five minutes of solid thought, I finally make my decision. There is no puma in there. It's just that Hastings wants me to think that there is a puma in there.

So I decide to enter the house, by breaking another hole in the now-replaced frosted-plate-glass window to the left of the front door. So I break out a small portion of this glass.

And I peer through this little hole I've made, and I see nothing. No puma. I listen. I don't hear any snarling cat or anything. No puma. Just the same, there *could* be a puma in there and it could be crouching silently just inside the door, waiting to pounce and bite my hand off when I put it in.

Very carefully, I put some fingers in and wiggle them. No puma. And so I put my arm in and reach and turn the doorknob from the inside and open the door a crack.

No snarl from a puma – whatever pumas snarl like. I open the door a little wider and I call, 'Here, pussy-pussy! Here, puma-puma! *Nice puma!*' No response.

I creep in very cautiously, looking around, ready to jump back and out and slam the door on this beast, if necessary. But there is no puma.

And then I realise that my decision was, of course, right, and there is no lousy puma in this damn house. But still, I am sweating like a pig and breathing heavily, and I suddenly figure out what Susie means when she talks about 'the power of the written word'.

With just a piece of writing, this Hastings transferred an idea from his crazy imagination into my mind, and I was willing to believe it.

So I walk down the hall to his bedroom door, which is shut, and there is another typed note on it.

Dear Burglar,

OK, so there is no puma. Did you really think I'd let a huge cat mess up my nice neat house?

However. I am going to give you a <u>serious warning</u>. DO NOT OPEN THIS DOOR! One of the engineers at our studio has invented a highly sophisticated security device and I've borrowed one of his models.

It's hidden in the bedroom and it works by means of ultrasonic waves. They are soundless and they have a fantastically destructive and permanent effect on brain tissues. It takes less than a minute of exposure.

You will not notice any brain-numbing effects at once, but in a few days your memory will start to go, and then your reasoning powers, and so, for your own sake,

DO NOT ENTER THIS ROOM

Harry Hastings

Well, I really had to hand it to this loony character. No wonder he made a lot of money as a writer. I, of course, do not believe *one word* of this, *at all*; therefore, I go into the bedroom and hurry to see if there is any hidden electronic device, but, of course, there is not. Naturally.

Then I see another note, on the closet door, and it says:

Dear Burglar,

I don't suppose I should have expected you to believe that one, with your limited imagination and your one-track mind. By the way, where do you go in all my clothes? You must be quite a swinger.

There are only a few new things in the closet. But before you take them, I suggest you sniff them. You will notice a kind of cologne smell, but this is only to disguise another odour. I have a pal who was in chemical warfare, and he has given me a liquid that can be sprayed inside clothing. No amount of cleaning can ever entirely remove it.

When the clothes are worn, the heat of the body converts this substance into a heavy gas that attacks the skin and produces the most frightful and agonisingly painful blisters, from the ankles to the neck. Never forget that you have been warned.

Harry Hastings

Well, I don't believe this for one moment, and so I open the closet door. All there is is one pair of slacks and a sports coat. But this coat looks like the very same *plaid cashmere* I took before and the rat stole from *me!*

But then I realise this could not be so, but it was just that Hastings liked this coat so much he went out and bought another just like it.

Anyway, I find myself sniffing these. They smell of cologne, all right, but nothing else, and I know, of course, that this kind of gas stuff does not exist at all except in Hastings's wild imagination, which I am coming to admire by now.

As I drive back to my pad, I start to laugh when I think of all the stupid and fantastic things that Hastings has tried to put into my mind today by the power of suggestion, and I realise that he almost succeeded. *Almost,* but not quite.

When I get home and climb the outside stairs to my front door, there are three envelopes taped to it, one above another. There are no names on them, but they are numbered, 1, 2, 3. I do not know what in hell all this could be about, but I open 1 and read:

Dear Burglar,

The plaid cashmere coat you have over your arm right now is not a replacement for the one you stole. It is the same identical coat. Think about this before you open envelope 2.

Harry Hastings

Well, of *course,* I think about this as I stand there with my mouth sort of hanging open. All of a sudden, it *hits* me! Harry Hastings was the rat who stole all his clothes back! But how did he know where I *live?* How could he know I was going to hit his house *today?* My hands are all fumbles as I open 2. Inside it says:

Dear Burglar,

To answer your questions. On your third visit to my house, my young neighbour saw you and followed you home in his car, and so found out just where you live. Later, in my own good time, I easily entered this place with a bent paper clip

The Harry Hastings method

and retrieved my own clothes. Today, my neighbour called me at my office and said you were inside my house again.

Later, I phoned him and he said you had come with my coat. So I've had time to come here and write and leave these notes. I also have had time to do something else, which you read about in 3.

Harry Hastings

I open this third envelope very fast indeed, because I figure that if Hastings knows all this, the fuzz will be along any minute. In it I read:

Dear Burglar,

I got the puma idea from a friend out in the valley who has one in a large cage in his yard. Long ago, I asked him if I might borrow this huge cat for a day sometime, and he said yes and that he didn't like burglars, either. He has a large carrying cage for the puma. I called him this morning the moment I heard you were inside my house, and he drove the puma right over here, and we released the huge cat inside your place. She is now in there, wandering around loose.

I have done this partly because I am vengeful and vindictive by nature and partly because I've made my living for years as a verisimilitudinous (look it up later) writer, and I deeply resent anyone I cannot fool. The puma that is now inside is my childish way of getting even.

This is no trick this time! If you have any brains at all, DO NOT OPEN THIS DOOR! Just get out of town before the police arrive, which will be in about half an hour. Goodbye. Harry Hastings

PS The puma's name is Carrie — as if that would help you any.

Well, I read in a story once where somebody was called a 'quivering mass of indecisive jelly', and that is what I was right then. I simply did not know *what* to think or believe. If this was any door but mine, I could walk away. But all my *cash* was hidden inside, and I *had* to get it before I could leave town …

I stand … I sweat … I think …

In your groups of three, come up with three different – but possible – endings for the story. Each person should report one of these to the class, saying what the evidence was for each choice.

Now read how Warner Law finished the story.

So I stand there and I sweat and I think and I think and after a long time, it comes to me that *this* time, Hastings is finally telling the *truth*. Besides I can hear little noises from inside. There *is* a puma in there! I know it! But I have to get *in* there, just the same!

I finally figure that if I open the door fast and step back, Carrie might just scoot past me and away. But maybe she will attack me.

But then I figure if I wrap the sports coat around one arm and the slacks around the other, maybe I can fend off Carrie long enough to grab a chair and then force her into my bathroom, the way lion tamers do, and then slam the door on her, and then grab my cash and run out of there, and the police can worry about her when they come.

So this is what I decide to do, only it is some time before I can get up the nerve to unlock the door and push it open. I unlock the door and I stand there. But finally, I think, 'Oh, hell, you *got* to do it, sooner or later,' and so I push my door open and stand back.

No puma jumps at me. Nothing happens at all. But then I look around the corner of my door and *Harry Hastings* is sitting inside. Not with a gun or anything. He is sitting very calmy behind the old card table I use as a desk, with a cigarette in his mouth and a pencil in his hand, and I see one of my stories in front of him.

I walk in and just stand there with my face on and cannot think of any clever remark to make, when he says: 'Tell me one thing. *Did* you or did you *not* really believe there was a puma in here?'

If I remember right – I was pretty shook up then – I nodded and I said, 'Yes, sir. Yes. I really did.'

Then he smiled a big smile and said, 'Well, thank heavens for *that*, I was beginning to think I was losing my grip. I feel a little better now. Sit down. I want to talk to you. By the way, your syntax is terrible and your grammar is worse. I've been making some corrections while waiting for you. However, that's not what I want to talk to you about. Sit down. Stop trembling, will you, and sit down!'

I sat.

As I write now, I am the co-owner and manager of the Puma Burglar Protection Agency. Harry Hastings is my silent partner and he put up two thousand dollars for financing. Susie helps me with my accounts. I have 130 clients now, at five dollars a month each.

The reason it's so cheap is that we use the Harry Hastings Method. That is, we don't bother with burglar alarms or things like that. I just patrol around and keep putting up and changing signs and notices and notes on front doors. Already, the burglary rate in my area has been cut by two-thirds.

This very morning, I got a little letter from Harry Hastings with two new ideas for front-door notes. One is: CLARA! I HAVE ALREADY CALLED THE POLICE AND THEY WILL BE HERE IN MINUTES! DO NOT CALL THEM AGAIN! GEORGE IS LOCKED IN THE BATHROOM AND CAN'T GET OUT, SO WE WILL BE SAFE TILL THEY GET HERE!

The second one is: NOTICE! BECAUSE OF A FRIGHTFULLY CONTAGIOUS DISEASE, THIS HOUSE HAS BEEN EVACUATED AND QUARANTINED. IT MUST ABSOLUTELY NOT BE ENTERED UNTIL IT HAS BEEN FUMIGATED!

Harry Hastings says that I should be sure to warn the householder to remove this notice before any large parties.

Warner Law

In your group, discuss what makes this a good, or a poor, ending. Think about your answers to these questions:

a How does Warner Law's ending compare with your versions?

b Was the ending a surprise?

c What makes this story typical of a 'crime' story?

On your own, write your answers to these four questions. Think carefully before you write and try to form an idea of what Harry is like in your mind.

a What *is* the Harry Hastings method?

b Why does Harry keep on writing notes to the burglar?

c Why doesn't he simply call in the police?

d Why does he decide to set up in business with the burglar?

2 Language and style

The success of this story is partly a result of the way in which it is written – its *style*. Warner Law is an American writer, and the burglar is going to a writing class. These two things affect how the story is told.

> With a partner, look at these statements about the story. Note down evidence from the story to support them.
>
> The burglar:
>
> **a** uses American words and the story uses American spellings ...
>
> **b** uses slang ...
>
> **c** writes in a conversational or colloquial way ...
>
> **d** is trying to improve the way he uses words ...
>
> **e** does not seem to understand how to paragraph his writing ...
>
> **f** uses different ways to emphasise what he wants to say ...
>
> **g** describes Harry in ways that show he admires things about him ...
>
> Report your findings to the class.
>
> Write a detailed character study of the burglar. Say what clues in the story help you to form a picture of him in your mind.

3 Adapting the story

What you have read is the burglar's story. Now, look at the story from another angle.

HAVE YOU GOT GOOD IDEAS YOU WOULD LIKE TO SEE IN FILM?

CAN YOU TRANSLATE WORDS INTO PICTURES?

Galloping Steed Studios has been asked to produce a series of short films for Channel 5 Television and is looking for new ideas. Send an outline of your ideas – in no more than five hundred words – to Betta Spelling, Galloping Steed Studios, The Old Workhouse, Cable Wharf, London E3.

> Write a letter to Betta Spelling in which you try to persuade her that *The Harry Hastings method* would make an excellent film for television.

... on adapting for television

To explain why a story would make a successful film you need to say something about:

1 The setting and the locations

Where will the film be set? In how many different places will the film be shot? Each new location adds a lot to the costs of a film.

2 Characters/casting

How many characters are needed? Which actors and actresses would be best suited to the roles? The more speaking parts there are, the greater the costs.

3 Dramatic possibilities

Where are the moments of real tension in the film? Where are the moments of decision? Is there a place for humour? Is the ending a surprise? How will it leave the audience feeling?

4 Potential problems

What parts of the story are likely to be hardest to film? How would you overcome these difficulties?

5 Target audience

Who is the film for? Children? Adults? School broadcasting?

on target

After working through this unit, could you:

- say what made a good crime story?

- talk about the style of writing in a story?

- discuss how to adapt a story for film or television?

It's the way that you say it

This unit explores the different varieties of spoken English and people's attitudes towards regional accents and dialect.

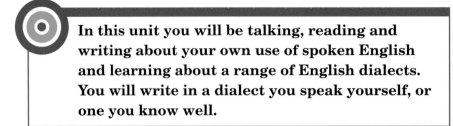

In this unit you will be talking, reading and writing about your own use of spoken English and learning about a range of English dialects. You will write in a dialect you speak yourself, or one you know well.

Making judgements

Talk about some of the experiences you have had in talking to people.

Have you ever:

a spoken to someone and decided whether or not you would get on with him or her because of the way he or she spoke?

b felt self-conscious, embarrassed or uneasy about the way you speak because someone you were talking to spoke in a different way?

c been teased or told off because of the way you speak?

d altered how you speak to impress other people or to be part of a group?

Look at the statements on the right.

Pick out one statement that you think is unfair and one that you think is true.

Explain the reasons for your opinions to the rest of your class.

What people say. Is it fair?

'Some accents are pleasant to listen to. Others sound horrible.'

'You can tell some people are clever by the way they talk.'

'People with posh accents are rich and snobbish.'

'Some accents are funny.'

'People with country accents are slow on the uptake.'

'Some accents make people sound thick.'

'Older people care more about the way you speak than young people do.'

'Not many people can speak correct English like they do on Radio 4. Most people make mistakes and say things wrong.'

'You can tell some people are really street-wise by the way they talk.'

'Some accents are better than others.'

2 How do you speak?

If you had lived in Great Britain about a hundred years ago, you would probably have spoken the dialect of the area you lived in, and you would have spoken it with a regional accent. But times change. Nowadays, we travel more. We move from one country to another, and from one community to another. We spend more time in school. We hear other ways of speaking on the television, the radio and in films.

All of these experiences influence the way in which we speak.

The films we watch, the music we listen to, the places we visit and the people we meet – all have an influence on the way we speak.

Skills Box

Spoken English

When talking about spoken English, there are three terms you need to understand:

Accent

This is the term used to describe the way people pronounce words.

Most British English speakers have a regional accent. The place they live influences the *sound* of their words.

Dialect

This is the term used to describe a different version of a language. Dialects have their own particular vocabulary (the words) and grammar (the way words are put together into sentences).

Dialects belong to particular places and are usually spoken with the accent of the same area. For example, Scouse dialect will be spoken with a Liverpool accent, Geordie dialect with a Newcastle accent.

Dialects also belong to particular cultures and communities. For example, the older members of some families may have come to Britain from another country, where English is not the first language spoken. It is quite possible that they will speak a very different form of English from other members of the family. The younger members will have spent all their lives in Britain and will have spoken English from their earliest childhood. Both their accent and dialect are likely to be different from those of their parents.

Standard English

This is the dialect of English used for most written English. It is a form of English speech that is taught all over the world. Very often, people switch between a local dialect and standard English when they need to. Standard English may be spoken with any accent.

What have been the influences on the way *you* speak?

Use the questions below to help you think about how you speak. Try to use the correct linguistic terms as you describe your accent and dialect:

- How has your family influenced your speech?
- How have the place (or places) where you have lived influenced your speech?
- Has your speech been influenced by contact with other dialects or languages?
- How have your friends influenced your speech?
- Has television or film affected your speech in any way?
- Have you ever consciously changed the way you speak?
- How would you describe the variety of English you speak?
- Do you like the way you speak now?
- Are there any reasons you might wish to alter the way you speak, either now or in the future?

Write an autobiographical piece of writing called 'My Language'. Write about your own language history and the events that have shaped the way that you speak now.

Start by writing about the dialect that your grandparents spoke or the main language of the place where you were born.

3 Changing how we talk

We all make choices about the way we speak. For example, we talk to friends rather differently from the way we talk to our family or teachers. Sometimes the differences are quite subtle, sometimes very noticeable. Developing your skills at switching from one variety of English to another – or from one language to another – to suit the situation is all part of being a good talker.

The text on the right lists a number of situations in which you would be expected to talk. In a small group, decide what is the appropriate way to speak for each occasion. Here are the possible choices you can make:

- I would speak as I normally do.
- I would make changes to my dialect.
- I would make changes to my accent.

Role play one of these situations with your group. First, use what you think is appropriate speech, then use a variety of spoken English which you think is inappropriate. The results should be funny!

Once you have practised your role plays, act the second one out to the rest of the class.

1 You are asked to show an important visitor round your school.

2 You need to return an almost new faulty personal stereo to a shop and ask for it to be replaced under the guarantee.

3 You are asked to read the news on national radio.

4 You are entertaining your friends with an account of a party you went to at the weekend.

5 You decide to put someone down who has been teasing you about your accent.

6 You are reading the weather forecast on breakfast television.

7 You have moved house to another part of the country, about two hundred miles away. In your class at your new school you are trying to get to know someone who seems to be very popular with the others.

8 A member of the Royal Family starts a conversation with you during a walkabout.

9 You are appearing on 'Blind Date' and you want to be the one who gets chosen.

10 You are invited to be guest DJ on your favourite radio music programme.

4 Dialect in fiction

Most of the books published in English are written in standard English. Authors sometimes, however, choose to write in dialect, either to show how their characters speak or to achieve a particular effect.

Read the following extract from *A Murder in Cornwall* by Gloria Cook with a partner or in a group. You will find writing in dialect is easier to understand if you bring it alive by reading it aloud.

A murder in Cornwall

Dinah Tredinnick has been murdered, and her maid has disappeared. At around the same time, a mysterious young girl, Kerris, who has lost her memory, arrives at Clem Trenchard's farm. Clem goes to Penzance to try to find out if there is a link between the two events.

Clem began his investigations by paying a visit to a popular local inn and listening in on the gossip there. It wasn't long before the horrific murders were mentioned and a rather hushed discussion was started.

A grim-faced sailor asked him, 'Know what we're talking about, do 'ee?'

'Aye,' Clem said, as if he was only half interested, as all faces turned to him. 'I come from further round the bay, two miles from Marazion. There's been some awful murders round there too over the past twenty-odd years. You must have heard about them.'

'Aye, we have,' the serving girl interjected. 'From what some folk do say, 'tes not only round the bay but up-along too.'

Clem gave an involuntary shudder. It made the business he was here on uncomfortably close to home. 'Makes you nervous for your kin, though 'tis only the immoral and low life being killed.'

'Not the last one!' exclaimed the landlord, slamming down tankards of frothing ale on the bar. He glared at Clem with hostility. There was bad feeling between Penzance and Marazion folk, ever since the former had ousted the latter as the principal market of the region. 'She were a good, decent little maid. Well brought up, she was. Her father's a silversmith. They got a nice little house up Caunsehead.'

Clem ignored the frostiness of the landlord. 'There's many theories going round to who the killer is. Some say he could be a sailor, begging your pardon,' he added to the first man who had spoken to him. 'They happen sporadically so it could be when a ship moors up here or at the Mount.'

'Aye, Penzanns is a seafront town, 'tes what most folk think 'ere too,' someone else said.

'Didn't one of the victims have a maidservant go missing? One who was never found?' Clem queried, glancing round at the men and the well-built serving girl who gave him a come-on eye.

'Why do 'ee ask?' the landlord spat, and Clem was suddenly surrounded by suspicious faces.

'No reason, forget I asked.' He scowled at them. 'Just being conversational.' He drank up and left. He couldn't tell anyone he suspected the missing

maid was living on his farm. If he spoke to the killer or someone who knew the killer, he would put Kerris's life, and possibly his family's, in terrible danger.

He wandered about Penzance, listening to talk among traders and customers around the Market House at the top of Market Jew Street and round the corner at Greenmarket.

Back in Chapel Street he made his way just a little further along, crossed the street and stopped by St Mary's Chapel, where a legless beggar hailed him. 'Got a penny for an old soldier, sir?'

Clem tossed the beggar, who may have been an old soldier but was not an old man, and unusually clean-looking for one of his trade, a shilling and crouched down to talk to him. 'Have you done well today?'

'Not too bad, thank 'ee, sir. A fine-lookin' gentleman just gave me a two-shillin' piece. My son and I will eat bread and meat tonight.'

'Where's your son now?'

'Oh, he's off lookin' fer any labourin' job he can do. He'll be back to pick me up on our cart, which is our home, hopin' I haven't fell foul of one of the constables and been locked up fer vagrancy.' The beggar pointed to the space where his legs should have been and grinned widely. 'I don't get too much trouble from 'em, 'tisn't as if they can put me in the stocks!'

'What's your name?' Clem asked.

'Jacob Penberthy and me son's called Ben. Got work fer him by any chance, have 'ee, sir? Ben's got a strong, broad back and I can turn me hands to anything, nothing wrong with them.' Jacob Penberthy held up two large calloused hands as proof of his statement.

'My name's Clem Trenchard and I'm the tenant farmer of Trecath-en Farm on the Pengarron estate, which is round the bay, past Marazion. I'm sure I can find something for you both for a few days and you're welcome to sleep in my barn. Tell me, Jacob, do you use this spot often?'

'Well, 'tes a rich man's street. If they'm in a generous mood I do quite well and the curate in there,' he thumbed towards the Anglican chapel behind him, 'I don't think he likes me being here but he rarely tells me to clear off. I do the rounds of the bay, been coming here fer years. Why yer asking?'

'Well, you must know about the gruesome murder of a woman in this very street recently.'

'Aye, Miss Tredinnick. She was some good to me, 'twas a terrible shame about she.'

'Do you remember Miss Tredinnick's maid? She disappeared on the night of the murder.'

'No,' Jacob Penberthy crushed Clem's hopes as soon as they were raised. 'They lived further up the street and I can't see folk coming and going up that far. I never did see Miss Tredinnick with anyone.'

'So you've no idea what the maid looked like or what she was called? From folk talking about it perhaps?'

'Weren't round here back in the spring when the murder happened and folk are reluctant to talk about such a terrible thing openly in case it brings 'em bad luck. But ... '

'But what, Jacob? Think hard.'

'Well, once or twice Miss Tredinnick mentioned the name Amy. That could be the maid, I s'pose.' Jacob looked keenly at Clem, glanced up and down the street and cautiously behind them. 'Think you know where she is, do 'ee?'

'I might, but 'tis better I don't say any more. The name might be useful though. I thank you, Jacob.'

Jacob eyed Clem and touched his arm. 'The gentleman who gave me the two shillings today asked me a few questions about Miss Tredinnick and her missing maid too.'

Clem felt real panic.

Gloria Cook (from *A Murder in Cornwall*)

Working with your partner, answer the following questions by looking closely at the text:

- In what way do you think Clem is different from the people he speaks to in Penzance?

- How does the writer give this impression?

5 Dialect in script

Playscripts are all dialogue, so playwrights pay careful attention to how their characters speak their lines.

Read this extract in a small group.

An unexpected visit

This script from *When Last I Did See You* by Liselle Kayla features Jamaican Creole – the form of English widely spoken in Jamaica. A Creole is a dialect that has developed so many rules of its own that it has almost become a separate language.

Claudia, Shirley and Lloydy are at home in London when their mother's old friend – Miss Mary – calls.

The family home, England

Claudia is lounging on the sofa absorbed in a black women's magazine. Shirley is at the table surrounded by textbooks, trying to do her homework while rhythmically rocking to a Five Star track. Enter Lloydy with ghetto blaster, blasting.

CLAUDIA: Turn that blasted thing off will you!

SHIRLEY: Yeah! How am I supposed to do my work through all that!

LLOYDY: (*not taking any notice*) Watch here, Shirley, watch dis! (*demonstrates the latest reggae dance he has been practising in his room*)

SHIRLEY: Turn it off, I'm trying to listen to my record.

LLOYDY: Cho! You waan listen to some Real music – dubstyle. (*turns up the volume. Shirley retaliates by turning up the player*)

CLAUDIA: (*sarcastically*) Why don't you two grow up! (*bell rings*) Turn it off! There's someone at the door!

They both oblige, and Lloydy opens the door to Miss Mary who is clasping a battered paraffin can and wearing a grim no-nonsense expression.

LLOYDY: (*aside, and none too pleased*) Oh no, it's Miss Mary. (*then loudly and with forced cheerfulness*) Oh hello, Miss Mary!

MARY: What happening inside de house? What a way unu carry on when unu have white people fe you neighbour!

LLOYDY: Is music, Miss Mary, music – and dem love it.

MARY: Love what? How anybody coulda love dat deh bangarang?

LLOYDY: But dem always bangin' on de wall when we stop, Miss Mary.

MARY: Stop you foolishness, boy! (*entering room*) Dat same music gwain bring down de price of you mother house if you don't watch you step.

LLOYDY: I was just telling Shirley to watch de same ting, Miss Mary!

MARY: Where she is? ... me not stopping.

LLOYDY: (*under his breath*) Oh good, Miss Mary.

MARY: What you say, boy? ... I was just on me way to buy some paraffin so I thought I would pass by and say howdy. Hello children.

CLAUDIA: Hello, Miss Mary. Mum's not here. She's gone down the high street to buy a pair of shoes.

MARY: Shoes again? But don't is only last month she buy a new-brand pair? Me can't understand how one somebody need so much shoes. Me done tell her already say she gwain wear out her foot-bottom before she wear out de amount of shoes she have.

CLAUDIA: Well, she'll be back soon. She went out about two hours ago.

LLOYDY: No she won't! She told me she was going out all day (*winking to Shirley*) – ennit, Shirl?

SHIRLEY: (*conspiring*) Yeah! You know what she's like when she goes shopping for clothes.

MARY: Well, I suppose I better not waste me time. Me haffe go back to work soon.

LLOYDY: Yea, that's right, Miss Mary, you don't want to waste your time.

MARY: (*noticing Shirley's books*) Shirley. You doing you schoolwork, child? Keep it up, de Lord know how you gwain need all de level you can get. What level you doing now?

SHIRLEY: Well it's like this Miss Mary – I scraped through me 'O' levels, only just. And now I'm scraping through me 'A' levels, but I'm getting stuck at the 'O' level part of the course.

MARY: (*impressed*) 'A' level and 'O' level! Yes, das what me did tink. Keep it up, you hear, girl? My big girl in Jamaica did do her exams and now she working in one ah de big-big bank in Orange Street. Every month she send letter, tell me how she getting on. Yes, keep up de good work, child. If me and you mother did have de same edication you pickney have today, we would never be in dis country. And me would still be wid me t'ree pickney. (*sadly*) Ai sah! Life Hard!

CLAUDIA: Don't you miss them, Miss Mary?

MARY: Of course me miss dem. But what fe do? (*sigh. Pause*) ... and Lloydy, what you doing wid yourself boy?

LLOYDY: Not'ing much.

MARY: Not'ing much? Boy don't stand here in front ah me and tell me say you doing 'not'ing much'. What you doing wid you under-ripe self now you tek it pon yourself fe leave school?

LLOYDY: Mekking music, Miss Mary – trying fe turn reggae superstar.

MARY: (*kissing her teeth scornfully*) Mekking music, me back foot! Why you can't go outta street fe find work, boy? If you did stop talking wid de bad English and start comb you head and fling 'way de old frowsy hat, you would find job. Next time me come here me waan fe hear say you working. You hear me, boy?

LLOYDY: (*saluting in mock respect*) Yes, Miss Mary. Anyt'ing you say, Miss Mary.

Liselle Kayla (from *When Last I Did See You*)

Check your understanding of the extract, and of the Jamaican Creole language used by Liselle Kayla.

a List ten dialect words or expressions used by Miss Mary and give their standard English translations.

b List ten words in the extract which are spelled differently from the usual standard English spelling in order to reflect the way she pronounces them.

c Apart from Miss Mary, who else in the play speaks in dialect? Why do you think this character chooses to speak in dialect?

d Which characters speak standard English? Why do you think they choose to speak like that?

6 Using dialect in your own writing

> Choose a dialect (not standard English).
> Write a scene from a television series
> which shows an argument during a
> family mealtime and includes the use of
> this dialect.

Follow these steps for success.

1 Create four or five characters – you could include a visitor

Note down names, ages and a few points about each personality. Remember, older people are more likely to speak a regional dialect than younger ones.

2 Decide upon four or five things the family will talk about

This could be a mixture of everyday experiences and one or two special or unusual happenings.

3 Build some conflict into your scene as you write the first draft.

4 Work with a partner to check each other's scripts.

Help each other by suggesting possible improvements. Then, produce a final draft of your script.

5 Read the final versions of the scripts you have produced out loud in small groups.

Make a tape of the best one from each group to play to the rest of the class.

... on how to set out a script

1 Begin with a list of characters and brief details about each one.

2 Start your play by setting the scene. Where is it? Who is on stage? What are they doing?

3 Set out the dialogue by writing the speaker's name in capital letters, followed by a colon and then the words they say. Start a new line for each new speaker.

4 Do not use speech marks in a script, but take great care to use question marks and exclamation marks where they are needed.

5 Use stage directions to show how someone says his or her words. Place these in brackets after the speaker's name.

6 Use stage directions in brackets or in between speeches to explain what characters do or to show when they enter and exit in the middle of speeches. Stage directions are sometimes written in a different type-face so that you can see they are not words to be spoken. If you are using a word-processor, you could use italics.

... on how to write dialogue which reflects dialect

1 Think carefully about the use of dialect words and try to use them accurately.

2 Decide when and how you will alter the spelling of words to reflect accent and how you will spell dialect words which are not used in standard English.

3 Think carefully about the situation and the characters you create and ask yourself whether regional dialect would be spoken by that person in that situation in real life.

4 Remember that this piece of writing is not intended to make fun of dialect speakers by parodying, caricaturing or stereotyping them. This happens so often on television that you may find it hard to resist, unless you are constantly aware of the danger.

 **on target**

After working through this unit, could you:

- tell the difference between an accent and a dialect?

- explain to a friend what standard English is?

- adapt the way you speak to suit a particular situation?

- recognise when a writer is using dialect in a play, story or poem?

- write in dialect when you include conversation in a story?

Good friends

What makes someone a good friend? Do your reasons for choosing someone as a friend change as you grow older? What makes some friendships last for a long time, while others fizzle out?

In this unit you will discuss your own ideas about friendship and compare your experiences with the way three authors wrote about friendships between characters in their novels. You will then write part of a story of your own.

What is friendship?

Make a copy of the chart below. Working with a partner of the same sex, decide how much importance you would give to each of these reasons for choosing a friend by ringing a number (5 = most important, 1 = least important). See how far you can agree. If you both think there are qualities missing that are important in a friend, add your own ideas to the list.

A good friend is ...

		5	4	3	2	1
1	Someone who likes the things you do.	5	4	3	2	1
2	Someone you admire.	5	4	3	2	1
3	Someone who makes you laugh.	5	4	3	2	1
4	Someone you can trust with secrets.	5	4	3	2	1
5	Someone who is easy to talk to.	5	4	3	2	1
6	Someone good looking.	5	4	3	2	1
7	Someone who is generous.	5	4	3	2	1
8	Someone who is sympathetic when you feel miserable.	5	4	3	2	1
9	Someone who is popular with others.	5	4	3	2	1
10	Someone who admires you.	5	4	3	2	1

Compare your list with another pair's list, preferably a pair of the opposite sex. In your group of four, discuss the reasons for any differences you find.

Share your conclusions with the rest of the class.

2 Friendships in literature

Tom Sawyer was first published in 1876. In this novel, Mark Twain tells how Tom and Huck become friends as they share a series of adventures. One of the most memorable episodes in the book involves an incident based on a real experience of the author's. As a boy, Mark Twain had witnessed a drunken stabbing.

In the book, the story runs like this: Tom and Huck are in a graveyard in the middle of the night. They see Dr Robinson together with two of the town's 'ne'er do wells': Muff Potter, who is drunk, and Injun Joe. These three are there to steal a body from a grave (doctors occasionally did this at the time in order to perform medical research, which was illegal). An argument starts, and the Doctor is stabbed by Injun Joe. Injun Joe then tries to convince his drunken accomplice that *he* was responsible.

From their hiding place, the two boys witness the whole incident. This extract shows how they react to what they have just seen.

> By and by their pulses slowed down, and Tom whispered:
>
> 'Huckleberry, what do you reckon'll come of this?'
>
> 'If Dr Robinson dies, I reckon hanging'll come of it.'
>
> 'Do you, though?'
>
> 'Why, I know it, Tom.'

Tom thought awhile; then said:

'Who'll tell? We?'

'What are you talking about? S'pose something happened and Injun Joe didn't hang, why he'd kill us some time or other, just as dead sure as we're a lying here.'

'That's just what I was thinking to myself, Huck.'

'If anybody tells, let Muff Potter do it, if he's fool enough. He's generally drunk enough.'

Tom said nothing – went on thinking. Presently he whispered:

'Huck, Muff Potter don't know it. How can he tell?'

'What's the reason he don't know it?'

'Because he'd just got that whack when Injun Joe done it. D'you reckon he could see anything? D'you reckon he knowed anything?'

'By hokey, that's so, Tom!'

'And besides, look-a-here – maybe that whack done for him!'

'No, 'tain't likely, Tom. He had liquor in him; I could see that; and besides, he always has. Well, when Pap's full, you might take and belt him over the head with a church and you couldn't phase him. He says so his own self. So it's the same with Muff Potter, of course. But if a man was dead sober, I reckon, maybe that whack might fetch him; I dono.'

After another reflective silence, Tom said:

'Hucky, you sure you can keep mum?'

'Tom, we got to keep mum. You know that. That Injun devil wouldn't make any more of drownding us than a couple of cats, if we was to squeak 'bout this and they didn't hang him. Now look-a-here, Tom, less take and swear to one another — that's what we got to do — swear to keep mum.'

'I'm agreed, Huck. It's the best thing. Would you just hold hands and swear that we — '

'Oh, no, that wouldn't do for this. That's good enough for little rubbishy common things — specially with gals, cuz they go back on you any way, and blab if they get into a huff — but there orter be writing 'bout a big thing like this. And blood.'

Tom's whole being applauded this idea. It was deep, and dark, and awful; the hour, the circumstances, the surroundings, were in keeping with it. He picked up a clean pine shingle that lay in the moonlight, took a little fragment of 'red keel' out of his pocket, got the moon on his work, and painfully scrawled these lines, emphasising each slow down-stroke by clamping his tongue between his teeth, and letting up the pressure on the up-strokes:

"Huck Finn and Tom Sawyer swears they will keep mum about this and they wish they may Drop down dead in their tracks if they ever Tell and Rot."

Huckleberry was filled with admiration of Tom's facility in writing and the sublimity of his language. He at once took a pin from his lapel and was going to prick his flesh, but Tom said:

'Hold on! Don't do that. A pin's brass. It might have verdigrease on it.'

'What's verdigrease?'

'It's poison. That's what it is. You just swaller some of it once — you'll see.'

So Tom unwound the thread from one his needles, and each boy pricked the ball of his thumb and squeezed out a drop of blood.

In time, after many squeezes, Tom managed to sign his initials, using the ball of his little finger for a pen. Then he showed Huckleberry how to make an H and an F, and the oath was complete. They buried the shingle close to the wall, with some dismal ceremonies and incantations, and the fetters that bound their tongues were considered to be locked and the key thrown away.

A figure crept stealthily through a break in the other end of the ruined building now, but they did not notice it.

'Tom,' whispered Huckleberry, 'does this keep us from ever telling — always?'

'Of course it does. It don't make any difference what happens, we got to keep mum. We'd drop down dead — don't you know that?'

Mark Twain (from *Tom Sawyer*)

105

Good friends

Check your understanding of what you have read.

Working with your partner, list all the things Tom admires about Huck and all the things Huck admires about Tom. Back up what you say with short quotations from the extract.

Use a copy of a chart like the one below to help you.

What Tom admires about Huck	
The evidence from the passage	
What Huck admires about Tom	
The evidence from the passage	

This story was written by an American writer one hundred years ago. List five short sentences or phrases from the story that help you to tell this and give your reasons for thinking so.

Use a copy of a chart like the one below to help you.

The phrase from the story	Why you think this phrase shows the book was written long ago
Tom's facility in writing and the sublimity of his language	This kind of language would not be found in a modern book. It means that Tom can write well and has a good command of language – although I'm not so sure that he has!

Good friends

Making friends – girls

This extract from *Jane Eyre by* Charlotte Brontë (written in 1846) comes from a part of the novel where Jane has been sent to Lowood School by her aunt. She does her best but is unjustifiably attacked by the bullying Mr Brocklehurst, who calls her a liar in front of the whole school.

Ere the half-hour ended, five o'clock struck; school was dismissed, and all were gone into the refectory to tea. I now ventured to descend: it was deep dusk; I retired into a corner and sat down on the floor. The spell by which I had been so far supported began to dissolve; reaction took place, and soon, so overwhelming was the grief that seized me, I sank prostrate with my face to the ground. Now I wept: Helen Burns was not there; nothing sustained me; left to myself I abandoned myself, and my tears watered the boards. I had meant to be so good, and to do so much at Lowood: to make so many friends, to earn respect, and win affection. Already I had made visible progress: that very morning I had reached the head of my class; Miss Miller had praised me warmly; Miss Temple had smiled approbation; she had promised to teach me drawing, and to let me learn French, if I continued to make similar improvement two months longer: and then I was well received by my fellow-pupils; treated as an equal by those of my own age, and not molested by any; now, here I lay again crushed and trodden on; and could I ever rise more?

'Never,' I thought; and ardently I wished to die. While sobbing out this wish in broken accents, some one approached: I started up – again

Helen Burns was near me; the fading fires just showed her coming up the long, vacant room; she brought my coffee and bread.

'Come, eat something,' she said; but I put both away from me, feeling as if a drop or a crumb would have choked me in my present condition. Helen regarded me, probably, with surprise: I could not now abate my agitation, though I tried hard; I continued to weep aloud. She sat down on the ground near me, embraced her knees with her arms, and rested her head upon them; in that attitude she remained silent as an Indian. I was the first who spoke –

'Helen, why do you stay with a girl whom everybody believes to be a liar?'

'Everybody, Jane? Why, there are only eighty people who have heard you called so, and the world contains hundreds of millions.'

'But what have I to do with millions! The eighty I know despise me.'

'Jane, you are mistaken: probably not one in the school either despises or dislikes you; many, I am sure, pity you much.'

'How can they pity me after what Mr Brocklehurst said?'

'Mr Brocklehurst is not a god: nor is he even a great and admired man: he is little liked here; he never took steps to make himself liked. Had he treated you as an especial favourite, you would have found enemies, declared or covert, all around you; as it is, the greater number would offer you sympathy if they dared. Teachers and pupils may look coldly on you for a day or two, but feelings are concealed in their hearts; and if

you persevere in doing well, these feelings will ere long appear so much the more evidently for the temporary suppression. Besides, Jane – '
She paused.

'Well, Helen?' said I, putting my hand into hers. She chafed my fingers gently to warm them, and went on –

'If all the world hated you, and believed you wicked, while your own conscience approved you, and absolved you from guilt, you would not be without friends.'

'No; I know I should think well of myself: but that is not enough; if others don't love me, I would rather die than live – I cannot bear to be solitary and hated, Helen. Look here; to gain some real affection from you, or Miss Temple, or any other whom I truly love, I would willingly submit to have the bone of my arm broken, or to let a bull toss me, or to stand behind a kicking horse, and let it dash its hoof at my chest – '

Charlotte Brontë (from *Jane Eyre*)

Check your understanding of what you have read.

a Note down four or five ways in which Helen demonstrates her friendship for Jane. Can you suggest why Helen is friendly to Jane?

b This is a story about a friendship between two girls. In your view, does it describe a typical female friendship?

c Jane Eyre's story, like *Tom Sawyer*, was written a long time ago – in 1846. List five short sentences or phrases from the story that help you to tell this.

Use a copy of a chart like the one below to help you.

The phrase from the story	Why you think this phrase shows the book was written long ago
Ere the half-hour ended	We don't use the word 'ere' any longer; we say 'before'.

Good friends

Making friends in a new town is never easy. In this extract from *The Red Ball* by Ismith Khan, Bolan's ability to play cricket helps him become part of a group.

'Aye ... Thinny Boney! You want to play?'

One of the boys called out to him, and although he had heard and knew that they were calling him, he kept pulling out the red petals of the hibiscus flower, tore off their bottom ends and blew into the fine pores of needle holes at the base until the petals swelled out into a thin balloon of pink skin which he pierced with the straight pin which kept his shirt front closed.

'Match-stick foot! You playin' deaf. You want to play or don't you want to play?'

In his childish way, the boy had understood that if he answered to any of the names they coined for him, he would have to live with it forever. For two weeks now, since they moved to Port of Spain he had been coming to Woodford Square in the evenings. At first he sat in the fountain with his thin long legs dangling in the water, the spray falling on his face, and when no one was going past he waded across the waist-high water to the green and mossy man-sized busts where there was the giant of a man standing lordly amid four half-fish half-woman creatures, a tall trident in his massive arm pointing to the shell of blue sky.

'Aye, you! What you name? You have a name or you ain't have a name?'

He looked at the boys through slitted eyes, still seated on the foot-high cement runner that ran around Woodford Square with tall iron rails pierced deep into the runner. On previous evenings, when the city workers were still wending their ways home through the short-cut square, he had stayed away from its centre and its fountain, catching flowers of the yellow and purple *poul* as they spun sailing earthward. He waited like a small animal scenting the wind with his nostrils until some small gust unhinged a flower and he went racing below the path it was slowly tracing as it came spinning and dancing slowly down to earth. During the past week he came and sat on the runner where the boys played cricket until the fireflies came out in the square and the boys went home with their bats and wickets and balls, then he got up and caught some fireflies and put them in a small white phial to put under his pillow so that he could watch them glow when they blew out the kerosene lamp.

'Aye – no name – what is your name?'

'I name Bolan,' he said sullenly as he eyed the six or seven boys who had stopped their game and stood about from their batting or bowling or fielding positions waiting on him.

'Well ... you want to play or you don't want to play? Cat bite your tongue or what?'

He still sat on the runner, his long-boned hands hung down between his knees, admitting to himself that the cricket set the boys had was good, three wickets made from sawed off broomsticks, which they had nailed into the ground, two bats, one made from a coconut branch, the other a real store bat that smelled of linseed oil, and a cork ball that had red paint on its surface. He rose, took up the ball, and began

hefting it, tossing it up in the air, then catching it to feel its weight, while the other boys looked on in silence.

In Tunapuna he had played with used tennis balls which rich people sold for six cents apiece after they had lost their bounce and elasticity. Only on Sunday matches had he seen a real cork ball and the touch of this one, its rough texture between his fingers, its very colour, gave him a feeling of power. He knew that he could bowl them all down for 'duck' with this ball.

The boys first looked at each other questioningly, then they began moving to their playing positions as they watched the thin boy count off fifteen paces. He turned and his feet slapped at the turf moving him along like a feather, his thin long body arched like a bow, the ball swung high in the air, his wrist turned in, and he delivered the shooting red ball that turned pink as it raced to the batsman. The batsman swiped blindly and missed, his head swung back quickly to see how the ball could have gone past him so quickly. 'Aye, I aye,' the wicket-keeper cried out, as the ball smacked into his hands making them red hot. The fielders who were scattered far off moved in closer to see if they could catch the secret in his bowling, but each time he sent the ball shooting through the air, they missed some small flick of his wrist that made him bowl them all down before they could see the ball.

'You want to come back and play tomorrow?' they asked as they stood about the corner of Frederick and Prince streets, eating black pudding and souse from a vendor who had a charcoal brazier going on the street corner.

Ismith Khan (from *The Red Ball*)

Check your understanding of what you have read.

a   Describe the events which lead up to Bolan's acceptance by the group.

b   How typical of boys, and of the sort of friendships they have, is what happens in this story?

c   What differences are there between this friendship and that between Helen and Jane?

3 Choose a fictional friend

Choose one of the characters described in these extracts. Write a letter to a real friend of yours explaining why you would like to have your chosen fictional character as a friend, either now, or when you were younger.

Follow these stages for success:

1 Sort out your ideas
Use the list of qualities you drew up at the start of the unit as a starting point for your writing. Then give examples from the extracts where your chosen character reveals those qualities. You may wish to make notes about:

* the way the person behaves

* things he or she says and does

* his or her personality

* his or her attitudes and opinions

* reasons you feel you would enjoy his or her company, and he or she would enjoy yours.

You could also note down any reservations you have about the character:

* If you feel he or she is too good to be true, explain why.

- Describe aspects of your chosen character, or of yourself, which you think could lead to a personality clash.

2 Drafting

Get your ideas down on paper. The different sections in your notes should help you organise your writing. Since this is a letter to someone you know well, the style can be fairly chatty and colloquial. You could begin by writing something like this:

I've just been reading a really good book, and there was someone in it who I would like to know in real life because s/he would be almost as good a friend as you are. I bet you would get on with him/her too!

3 Revising and redrafting

Read your work through and decide how you can:

- add to the ideas

- reorganise ideas

- express what you have written better

- improve on spelling and punctuation.

Remember to set out the final draft as a letter, with your address and date correctly set out at the top.

on target

After working through this unit, could you:

- tell someone what, in your view, makes a good friend?

- compare the friendships described in two stories you have read yourself?

- write a story about a childhood friendship?

- tell who your real friends are?

Driven to the limits

In 1990, almost 40% of people involved in the theft of cars were under 17. Recent studies have shown that most so-called joyriders start taking cars between the ages of 13 and 15, with passengers as young as 10 years of age. What makes young people break the law in this way and put themselves and other innocent people in such danger?

 In this unit you will think about and discuss these issues as you plan and write a story about a young person who becomes involved in this dangerous 'game'.

1 Starting your story

To write a story, you have to understand the background to it. For this story, you need to know what motivates people, or makes them do what they do.

Working as a small group, discuss what you know about young people and car theft.

Have you:

- seen items on television news bulletins?

- read newspaper stories?

- been talked to at school?

- known anyone involved?

- heard any stories?

What is your opinion of people who steal and drive cars? Why do they do it? What consequences usually follow?

Report back your group's opinions to the rest of the class.

2 Create a character

Now, in your group, discuss the character of a typical juvenile car thief. Draw up a 'profile'. Collect information under headings such as:

Age
Sex
Background
Character/Personality
Hobbies/Interests

You could add a 'police photograph', too, like these.

HAVE THE LAST LAUGH.
SECURE YOUR CAR.

FIGHT BACK.
SECURE YOUR CAR.

3 Develop the plot

Stories deal with a series of events. They involve characters who cause things to happen, or to whom things happen.

In your story, you are going to have to describe what leads up to the theft of a car and what happens afterwards.

Here is a list of events that could lead up to the theft of a car. Can you add to these ideas?

Discuss them with your group and try to add at least one new idea each.

- An argument at home

- Being told off or made to feel stupid at school

- Trying to impress mates or a girl

- Daring one another to do things

- Finding a car with a window open

Here is a list of some of the things that happen when young people steal cars. What can your group add to this list?

- Innocent people are killed or injured.

- Children and the elderly are particularly at risk.

- The cars skid while being driven at speed, and the drivers lose control.

- Cars are dumped or set on fire.

- There are high-speed chases involving police cars.

- Passengers can be killed or injured.

Share the best new ideas from each group with the rest of your class.

Think about the plot of your story. What is going to happen to *your* character? Briefly note down the main events in your story.

As a group, compare your plot outlines. Help each other by suggesting improvements or new ideas.

TiPS ...

... on plots and sub-plots

1. **Make your plot interesting by introducing some unexpected elements**
Think about the passengers and why they are in the car. Think about other characters – the victims, the driver's best friend, his or her teachers, his or her parents, the police involved in the story.

2. **Think about having a sub-plot**
A sub-plot is a minor story which unfolds alongside the main story. A sub-plot can help you to vary the pace and the drama of your story. It allows you to present the events of the main plot in a different context and to widen the scope of your story.
You can also use a sub-plot to make an additional comment on the main plot.

4 Start to tell your story

Deciding *how* to tell your story, what position to tell it from, is very important. With your group, look at the Skills box on narrative viewpoints (over the page) and discuss the advantages and disadvantages of writing from different viewpoints.

Finally, decide which viewpoint you will choose to tell your own story from.

Skills Box

Narrative viewpoints

Viewpoint 1: third-person narrative

Often a story is told by the writer who looks in on the events. This is called a third-person narrative. It is the way in which people naturally tell stories to children:

Dennis Collins was never happy after his mum and dad split up and he had to move to Clifton. The town seemed too small after Liverpool, and his mum was always out working at the cake factory. He found it hard to settle at school where the other children ignored the quiet, scruffily-dressed kid they called 'Scouser'.

Viewpoint 2: first-person narrative

Sometimes a story is told by someone who is part of the story. This is called a first-person narrative:

I hated the new school. The other kids were just country bumpkins in comparison with my mates Scarface and Dogear from Kirkby. They tried to be tough, but they just weren't up to it. They called me 'Scouser' – original or what? It was so boring that when I saw the red Porsche 944, I knew I had to have it.

Viewpoint 3: indirect first-person narrative

A similar technique is to tell events through the first-person narrative of another person in the story. This is called an indirect first-person narrative:

I didn't like the way the other kids treated 'Scouser'. It was in history when he spoke to me. We were finishing some homework and he turned round from the other table where he was sitting on his own and said, 'Can I borra yours?'

I didn't really think, just passed the exercise book over. At the end of the lesson, he passed it back. He just quietly passed it back without a word. I liked that. Then, after the bell went and we were streaming out through the scuffed door-frame, he came alongside me out of nowhere.

'Fancy goin' for a ride after?' he said. 'Meet you on the bridge, Mo.' I was surprised. I didn't think he even knew my name.

Viewpoint 4: flashback

Another way to tell a first person narrative is to use a flashback, where the person telling the story looks back on events from a later time:

I was sorting out some old drawers when I found the photograph. It was a surprise that I still had it. I was given it by his mother. I don't know why really, after what he did to me. Maybe she wanted to make amends in some way. It took me back to Year 9 at Kirkby High and the summer when everything changed ...

Viewpoint 5: multiple narrative

It is nowadays popular to have more than one narrator, so that different sections of the story are told by different people. This is called a multiple narrative:

We were on the quiet shift that day – the 2 'til 10, we called it. I saw the red Porsche first, about three minutes after we got the message to watch out for it. We would have clocked it anyway. It was going too fast, and the gears were racing as it shot past the turning where we were parked.

'Here we go,' said Kev, flicking on the lights and the klaxon at the same time, as he pulled into a gap in the traffic ...

Marge Bennett was in a hurry and had tumbled Tramp and Sherri into the car in a rush to get to the supermarket before Don came home. He was always teasing her about her absent-mindedness, and she didn't want him to know she had forgotten the chicken breasts for dinner ...

Dennis didn't have time to react. He knew he was going to jump the lights from way back, knew they were going to be red. They always were. That was what made it good, made your head buzz as if you were twice as alive as usual. The girl was scared. He could tell that by the way her hand was gripping the edge of the seat.

The impact came as a surprise. This was harder and different from what he had expected. The bonnet folded, the windscreen shattered in an instant. The girl's scream stopped suddenly, and it all went quiet. There was a hiss of steam as the radiator burst ...

Kev was already on the radio as I ran towards the cars. The red Porsche had swung round and there was steam coming from the radiator. The little car was upside down and by the swinging door was what looked like a pile of rags on the tarmac. I saw there was a woman and another child twisted across the front seat. I knew at once that she was dead.

Films and television programmes often use a multiple narrative. The pictures here represent one possible storyboard for the incident on the previous pages.

You should now be ready to write the first draft of your story. If you are handwriting your story, leave space in your margins to redraft and revise what you have written. If you are working on a word processor, make sure you save your story at regular intervals and keep any printouts.

5 End your story

You probably already have a good idea of how your story will end. But if you want your story to feel *real*, it must have an ending that might *really* happen.

> Discuss the endings of each of your stories with your group. Are they believable?
>
> Think about these points as you consider the closing events of your stories:
>
> * Many car thefts end in disaster, with people maimed or in hospital.
>
> * Car chases can be so dangerous that, in some areas, the police decide not to get involved in them.
>
> * People who steal cars are committing the offence of aggravated vehicle taking. For this they can receive up to two years in jail. If they cause a death, they can be given a sentence of up to five years in jail, an automatic driving ban and an unlimited fine.
>
> * Young offenders (those who are under fourteen) cannot be sent to prison. They can, however, be taken into care and put in an institution that is like a prison. They may also be sent to projects where they can learn about car maintenance and safe driving.

TiPS ...

... on how to write endings

Ending with an *afterword* can be very powerful

An afterword, as the name suggests, takes place some time after the main events of a story. It is a particularly useful way of drawing together the stories of each narrator in a multiple narrative. Here is an example:

On 5 June 1993, at Clifton Magistrates Court, fourteen-year-old Dennis Collins was sentenced to one year in prison, fined £500 and banned from holding a driving licence for ten years after admitting aggravated vehicle taking and five other motoring offences.

Don Bennett and his daughter Sherri have still not come to terms with what happened. Sherri often asks for her mother.

Maureen Draycott needed forty-eight stitches in her face. She cries a lot as well.

6 Redrafting, proof-reading and the final version

This is the stage where you can make major improvements to the story.

Work with a partner to discuss the strengths and weaknesses of each other's stories. Start with changes that might need to be made to the whole story, for example:

- If the plot is too predictable, or if you think the story is too short to be effective, then it might be a good idea to introduce a sub-plot and weave another story around it.

- If the writing seems dull and too detached, change the narrative viewpoint so that someone else tells the story. Make sure that characters' thoughts and feelings are conveyed, as well as what happens.

- If you do not include dialogue, it makes it difficult to explain why your characters do things. Try introducing new characters who ask them questions and force them to make statements!

- If the story doesn't seem to hang together, or the ending seems to happen too quickly, add events to fill the gaps.

When you are satisfied that you have made all the changes that need to be made to the story as a whole, move on to check that:

- You are making good use of description – of people, of places, of events.

- There is plenty of realistic dialogue.

- Details like the make of cars, people's names and clothes and the days of the week stay the same.

Finally, check and correct:

- your spelling

- your paragraphing

- the punctuation of dialogue.

Keep your work neat as you write the final version of your story, but don't be afraid to make changes even as you work. Give the story a title and draw an illustration to go with it.

7 Afterword

The term 'joyriding' is only used once in this unit. Can you think of some reasons why?

Can you think of a new word which sums up the activity better?

To help you, read the article below. It is not a story.

Deadly consequences

An ex-joyrider tries to explain the lure of the road and a bereaved mother describes the tragedy that can follow.

Stuart was 14 when he first had the urge to jump into a car – anyone's car – and drive it away. 'I'd got a Saturday job on a scrapyard, and I used to muck about in the old bangers,' he said. 'Then I started breaking into cars and driving them away with my mates. I used to watch my dad driving. I'd watch his feet really closely. It was easy to learn.'

Like most joyriders, Stuart fancied himself as an expert driver and a match for the police. But although he is now in his mid-20s, he still does not have a licence. He remains disqualified because of his long list of motor-related convictions.

'First I got caught for under-age driving. Then I had an accident – not a bad one – and got cautioned. When I was 17 I was sent to a young offenders' centre for four months. I gave it up for a while and even got a job.

'But I've always been car mad. I've had loads of sentences for car crimes – theft, unauthorised taking, you name it. None of them put me off.'

Stuart describes his family background in Derby as a happy one. But he hated school and hated working for £25 a week on a training scheme.

'I lost interest. I wanted to be out with the lads. I spent my sixteenth birthday driving down the motorway at 130mph, with nine of us in a stolen car egging each other on. It's difficult to describe the feeling you get. I suppose it's about being in control of that much power.

'We used to get a real kick out of giving the Old Bill a chase. You didn't think about the risks to yourself or anyone else.'

Stuart eventually gave up joyriding and other car crime. 'I got married, and had kids. When the probation services gave me a chance to go straight by going on a motor project, I took it. I've ended up a volunteer instructor on the Leicester

Action for Youth Trust motor project, teaching other ex-offenders how to do up cars and race them.

'I'm living on benefit, and I resent the fact that I'll never own a flash motor. But at least I think I've got the joyriding thing out of my system.'

It is just over a year since Carol Whittingham's 27-year-old son Steven was killed in a collision with joyriders.

'It was around 7.20pm. We think Steven had just popped out to put some petrol in the car. He'd even left the TV and fire on.'

The crash happened just 20 metres from his home, in Brighouse, West Yorkshire. 'A car came down the hill on the wrong side of the road at an

estimated speed of 80mph. It hit Steven's car head-on. He didn't have a chance. The car thieves' vehicle ended up in a playground where it burst into flames, trapping them inside.'

The joyriders escaped thanks to a friend of Steven's who ran out of his nearby shop with a fire extinguisher. 'They got out and legged it, leaving my son for dead. Steven's friend only realised later what had happened. He's a nervous wreck as a result.'

She adds: 'It was an 18-year-old driving the stolen car, with a 13-year-old on board. They caught them later. We think it was when the driver showed up for treatment at the hospital to which my son was taken. The 18-year-old came up for trial at Leeds Crown Court. He's got two previous convictions for joyriding, and pleaded guilty. All he got was three years' youth custody, which means he'll be out in a few months' time. The younger one is a habitual car thief, but he'll not go before the courts, of course.'

For Carol Whittingham, her husband and their three surviving children, the trial was a travesty. 'They should call it "deathriding", not "joyriding". We end up serving the life sentence. In court they didn't even made a reference to what we're suffering.'

She says that she now suffers from phobias, such as not being able to close the bedroom door because she was in bed when the crash happened. 'Yet despite all this you have to carry on.'

The Whittinghams have received support from a new national organisation, Roadpeace, which offers help to the relatives and friends of people killed on the road. Carol Whittingham is now helping set up a local branch in Yorkshire.

'We also need more support from parents who suspect their children might be involved in joyriding, but have no one to turn to. After all, how many of them are going to grass up their own kids to the police?'

(from *The Guardian*, 2 February 1993)

on target

After working through this unit, could you:

- plan a new story on another topic or issue without so much help?
- tell the difference between the narrative stances you meet in your reading?
- advise a friend about the dangers of stealing cars?

Animal crackers

Animal rights have become a major issue of the late twentieth century. Should we support factory farming because it produces cheaper food? Are zoos cruel? Should we allow the use of animals for medical research?

In this unit you will investigate two aspects of animal rights. Should people use animals for entertainment? In what conditions should we keep the animals we rear for eating?
You will discuss the issues involved and read some persuasive writing before writing an article of your own to encourage other people to share your views.

Look at what happens to animals

The table on this page lists a number of things that humans do to animals.

Discuss the list below with a partner.
Note what *you already know* on to a copy
of the table.

The activity	What is involved?	What is the law?	What is the purpose of the activity?	How does the activity affect the animals?
Fishing				
Keeping animals in 'factory' farms				
Hare coursing				
Rearing wild animals for fur				
Badger baiting				
Bear baiting				
Using animals for scientific research				
Dog fighting				
Using ferrets to catch rabbits				
Deer hunting				

List some questions that you will need to ask in order to check the *facts* about any of the activities listed. For example, you may not know whether some of these things are legal, or whether animals are harmed during the activity.

Join with another pair to make a group of four. Take it in turns to go through the questions you have listed. Then, choose two questions which the whole group would like to put to the class.

As you talk, and find out more, add new information to your grid. If your class cannot provide the information, consult reference books in the library to see if you can find the information there.

2 Find out more about an issue

Choose one of the activities from your list to research.

This activity could be something you are already strongly in favour of, or something you are firmly against. It could be something you feel has good arguments on both sides.

When you have completed your research, this will be the topic you will write about.

First, you need to find out more information. To do this, write a letter to one of the organisations concerned with the proper treatment of animals or animal rights.

PLEASE HELP STOP THIS

... on where to start looking for information

You will be able to find local addresses by looking up Animal Welfare Associations in *Yellow Pages*. You could also:

- look through reference books and directories in your school and local library

- watch out for articles in newspapers and magazines

- talk to friends and relatives about organisations of which they are members.

... on how to write letters to find out information

- Check with others in your class to find out who is writing to which organisation. Send your letters in one envelope, to save an organisation the expense of sending each of you separate information.

- Make sure your letter is correctly set out and clearly worded, so that whoever opens it can see quickly what information you want.

- Be completely precise about what you want to know. That way, you are more likely to receive appropriate materials in reply.

- Enclose a large stamped addressed envelope.

- Make sure your envelopes are clearly and correctly addressed.

- If you decide to send for information which you have to pay for, enclose a cheque or postal order for the correct amount, and make clear that you have done so in your letter.

King George V Secondary School
Warminster Road
Greater Cheshunt
Middleshire
MX2 5GU

24 May 1995

Dear Sir/Madam
I wonder if you could help me with some research I am doing for my English class.

I am a Year 9 pupil at King George's and we are looking at the way animals are treated in this country and all over the world. The book we are using has some really nasty pictures of bears being baited and attacked by dogs, and my teacher tells me that the pictures came from your organisation.

If she is right, I would be very grateful if you could give me some more information about bear-baiting. For instance, what countries allow this so-called sport? Where do the bears come from? How are they treated, before and after the baiting sessions? Do they always die? What is done with their bodies afterwards? Is there anyone I can write to to protest about this?

I would be really grateful if you could give me as much information about bear-baiting as you can.

Thank you very much for taking the time to read this letter.

Yours sincerely

Hassan Pelati (Year 9)

Skills Box

Researching an issue

You will be asked to research information on a particular topic as part of your work in many subjects at school. Successful research:

- starts with a clear question

- looks for the answer in the right places

- and keeps the new information in an organised way.

Follow these steps for success:

1 Decide what you want to know

When you start to research a subject, set yourself a specific question that you want answered, for example:

– What happened in the Great Fire of London?

– Why were so many new towns built after 1945?

2 Start with what you know

Note down what you already know about the topic you are researching. Talk about the topic with friends.

3 Begin in the library

Libraries are the places to start looking for new information. There are various places to start your search:

The subject indexes

These may help you find books that deal with particular themes. You would find books on history, geography or the environment, for example.

Keyword searches

Computerised indexes will let you enter a word or a phrase and then provide a series of references. Always choose as specific a word or phrase as you can.

CD-Roms

CD-Roms are computer disks that hold vast amounts of data. Always use the index or key words to help you search. Note down where you found useful information (i.e. a page number or section reference) as you work.

Encyclopaedia

An encyclopaedia may be a good place to start looking for information if you are unsure about exactly what you need to know. It will also give you good ideas for keyword searching.

Newspapers and magazines

Many libraries keep copies of newspapers and magazines either as old copies or on CD-Rom. These may be able to give you up-to-date information about a topic.

Addresses

There is almost certainly an organisation that publishes material related to your topic. It could be a charity, a fund-raising group, an awareness-raising group or a pressure group. Libraries often keep directories with their addresses in. Alternatively, they may have copies of leaflets on display.

4 File your information

As you find useful information which you may wish to use later in your written work, you need to organise it. Make sure that you note down the titles of:

- books, newspapers and leaflets where you found useful information

- television and radio programmes, together with a summary of what they were about

- any articles, pamphlets, tapes or videos you have collected.

3 Looking at persuasive writing

The information you are sent will often put forward views that are designed to influence the reader. The two pieces of writing below, about turkey farming, use the same kind of information, but they treat it differently in order to influence the reader's point of view.

Read these two articles with a partner.

Keep on gobbling!

Turkey is one of the healthiest, most economical and versatile meats available, and every year around eleven million cooked turkeys grace the Christmas dinner tables. More than a third of all the turkeys consumed annually are eaten between Christmas and the new year.

Although we take the Christmas turkey for granted, only forty years ago Christmas dinner was missing this traditional and popular element. The high cost of turkey meant it was a luxury that only the wealthier families could afford. Since then the development of modern farming methods has allowed this efficient industry to supply more turkeys at lower prices throughout the year.

The development of frozen storage facilities now allows farmers to make use of turkey sheds for twelve months a year. Previously, most farmers reared turkeys only in the six months leading up to Christmas. As a result of the new freezing facilities, output has doubled, and there has been only a small increase in costs. The shopper has benefited from price reductions, and sales have soared.

Other innovations in farming practice and transportation have combined to make the turkey industry even more cost effective. One of the most important changes has been the introduction of intensive farming methods.

These involve the rearing of large numbers of animals in relatively small indoor spaces.

The aim is to produce the largest possible quantity of meat in the shortest time. Large numbers of birds are kept in a relatively small space. They grow larger, and quicker, as they use up less energy on moving around and searching for food. These methods benefit the public by allowing more meat to be produced at lower cost to the farmer, thereby keeping prices in the shops low.

The second big change was that farmers began breeding especially large sizes of turkey. This was done by selecting the heaviest birds and mating them with each other. The result has been larger and heavier birds, which produce more meat. Today the average turkey produces twice as much meat as those of the 1950s.

Without these developments, thousands of people would have been unable to afford to eat turkey. The rearing of greater numbers of heavier turkeys has led to a dramatic fall in prices. Free range turkey costs about 90p per kilo, but birds reared in larger intensive sheds cost only half the price.

Turkey-farming is not cruel. It is regulated by a government code of practice. The ministry of agriculture sends veterinary inspectors to check farms, and, if farmers are causing 'unnecessary pain or distress' to their animals, they can be prosecuted.

Turkey farming or turkey **torture?**

In 1993, a total of 32 million turkeys were slaughtered, earning £287 million for the turkey industry, but at what price for human dignity? Chickens' Lib — a group that campaigns for animal rights in the poultry trade — criticises the methods by which turkeys are reared. It argues that many turkey farms are 'cruel, squalid and a danger to human health'. The criticisms are aimed at intensive 'factory farming' methods, commonly used by turkey farmers, that involve the rearing of a large number of turkeys in a tiny space.

The animal-rights campaigners say that the turkeys, in common with many other farm animals, are kept in unnatural conditions which cause them considerable stress and pain. They point out that turkeys grow so quickly today that they suffer from a range of physical ailments. Many are unable to walk properly because their legs cannot support their body weight. Older birds, for example, can reach as much as 36 kg. Common problems are deformed or fractured bones, slipped tendons, arthritis and foot ulcers.

Turkeys are by nature very active birds. They like to forage for food in the undergrowth. In confined spaces they quickly become frustrated and can become violent towards one another. At worst, they peck at each others' eyes and feet and can kill.

To prevent these attacks, many farmers use a hot blade to remove a section of the upper beaks of young birds when they are only a few days old. They may also blunt the tip of the lower beak. Animal-rights campaigners say this 'debeaking' is cruel and that it causes prolonged pain.

Most turkey farmers breed turkeys through a process known as artificial insemination. Sperm is removed from the male and introduced into females through a tube. Alastair Mews, head of the RSPCA's farm animals department, says the reason for this practice is that male turkeys grow so large that a female cannot support their weight during mating. 'People are breeding monsters which can no longer even reproduce naturally,' Mr Mews says.

Turkey farming is regulated by a government code of practice that states that a farmer can be prosecuted for causing unnecessary pain or distress to their animals. However, Chickens' Lib argues that farmers are very rarely prosecuted. The ministry of agriculture has prosecuted only three times in the past fifteen years!

With a partner, compare the way that these two articles set out to make the reader think differently about buying and eating turkey. Use a copy of the chart below to help you.

	Keep on gobbling!	Turkey farming or turkey torture?
In a short sentence, what do you think the main aim of the article is?		
Where does the article mention money? What does this show the reader?		
What details of turkey rearing does the article leave out?		
Where do the two articles use the same facts, but interpret them differently?		
Where does one article say one thing and the other make the opposite point?		
What adjectives (describing words) are used to describe the new farming methods?		
What organisations, people and authorities are used to back up the arguments?		

4 Your turn to persuade

> Write a piece of persuasive writing based on the research you have conducted into one of the activities listed on page 127.
>
> Produce an article for your school magazine or your local paper about the subject you have researched. The article should be around 400 words in length.

Follow these steps to success:

1 First draft

Select the most important or relevant information from all that you have found out. Go through your file, rereading the information you have collected. Use a highlighter pen to mark the points you want to make.

- Summarise in your own words the points you want to make. Some word-processors have a program that helps you make notes.

- Don't waste time by copying out opinions or examples in your notes. Instead, jot down where the evidence can be found when you write your article.

- Decide on an order for writing about the points you wish to make. Number them on your summary.

- Remember how important the beginning of a piece of writing is. Experiment by writing two or three different opening paragraphs and discuss with a partner which one is most effective.

Make a first attempt at writing what you want to say. Use your notes to guide you. At this stage, saying what you want to say is the most important thing.

- Read your work through and decide whether your ideas are in the best possible order. Do your points follow on logically from what went before? If not, does the sequence need to be altered?

- Check the length of your piece of writing. Consult a partner about how you can cut it down, if it is too long, or where you need to add more ideas, if it's too short.

2 Redrafting

At this stage you need to pay special attention to how your ideas are expressed. A newspaper or magazine article should be written in formal standard English, except where you are quoting words people actually said to you.

3 Proof-read

Once you have completed the draft, check it and correct slips in spelling, punctuation and paragraphing. Again, it will help if you discuss your work with your partner. You need to decide on the title for your writing.

4 The finished article

You know what you want to say and how you want to say it. Now concentrate on the presentation of your article. If you are using a word-processor, this is the point at which you can decide on the layout, size and type of font and overall appearance of your work.

Make any last-minute alterations to expression, spelling, paragraphing and punctuation before you commit your work to paper.

Make sure that any handwriting is a sample of your work at its neatest.

on target ?

After working through this unit, could you:

- take part in a class debate on another aspect of animal exploitation?

- write off to obtain information on another subject?

- produce a piece of writing based on your own research into a different subject?

- help a friend to make his or her writing more persuasive?

Glossary

The words listed here all appear in this book and are all used in English lessons.

This glossary helps you to understand what these words mean and gives you an idea of how you can use them.

The word		What it means
abstract	=	something that cannot be measured. Abstract nouns (beauty, anger, idea) describe things that cannot be observed or measured. Concrete nouns, as their name suggests, describe things that can.
accent	=	the way in which words are pronounced. Accents change from region to region, but the introduction of travel and television means that the differences between them are becoming less obvious. All languages are spoken in a variety of accents.
adaptation	=	turning something written in one medium (drama, print, film, music) into another. Books are adapted into films or plays and vice versa.
afterword	=	a short section at the end of a story or play, sometimes called an epilogue, that adds to the story, or rounds off the plot with extra information about the characters.
anthropomorphism	=	giving human characteristics and feelings to animals in stories
archaic	=	words (thou, hath, forsooth, upon my word) that are no longer used in normal language but found in older texts or are, sometimes, used for effect.
audience	=	the people who listen to what you say or read your writing. Your audience may be people you know or people you do not know. You have to think about who your audience will be as you plan what you want to say.
body language	=	a name for nonverbal communication – giving a message using the body rather than words. Holding a finger to the lips to indicate silence is an example.
bold type	=	a special effect in printing where letters are made thicker and darker on the page for emphasis. This is **bold** print. It is used in this glossary to make you notice key words.
brackets	=	also known as parentheses, brackets are placed around information that is separate from the main message of a sentence. Taking out the words in brackets should not change the meaning of a sentence.
caricature	=	a way of describing a character by exaggerating one or two features of appearance or personality.
character	=	a person in a story or play.
climax	=	the dramatic or exciting conclusion towards which events in a story, or a plot, build up
closed questions	=	questions that have one obvious or clear answer. 'How old are you?', 'Where do you live?' are examples.

The word		What it means
Creole	=	a language dialect (often a mixture of two languages) that has then become the mother tongue, or main language, of an area.
dialect	=	a different variety of the language of a country. A dialect has its own words (vocabulary), word order and grammar. It is often connected with one particular region. In English, many regional dialects are used in speech, but most writing uses standard English. As with accents, the differences in dialects are becoming less obvious.
dialogue (monologue)	=	a conversation between two people, spoken or written. A monologue is where only one person speaks – in a play, film or story.
draft	=	the first (rough) version of a piece of writing. It is sometimes written as notes or a plan.
exclamation mark	=	the punctuation mark (!) that shows when the preceding word has an extra emotional meaning. Exclamation marks are common in headlines, advertising and where direct speech occurs in stories.
fable	=	a short story, usually told about animals, with a moral. Aesop is the best known writer of fables but *Tom and Jerry* cartoons are a modern equivalent.
fantasy	=	imaginative writing that describes events and things that are completely out of the ordinary. Stories about ghosts and the supernatural, fairies, or space monsters, or children with special powers are all fantasies.
flashback	=	a narrative technique where a character 'remembers' events and describes them. Flashbacks are more common in film and television series than in books.
font	=	see typface
improvise	=	making up a play scene on a particular subject or theme 'as you go along'. Most improvisations are done in groups.
italic	=	a common text effect where the typface is *slanted like this*. Italics are often used for titles, foreign words or words that are referred to somewhere else in a book.
layout	=	the arrangement of words, or words and pictures, on a page. You talk about layout mostly when you are writing about posters, magazines and leaflets or experimenting with desktop publishing.
logo	=	the icon used by a company to link its products together. A logo is a visual symbol chosen by a company (or another organisation) to represent its image.
lower case	=	a name for small letters like these that are not capitals (upper case).
lyric	=	a name for a short verse or rhyme. Song lyrics are the best known examples.
narrator	=	the person who tells the story in a novel or short story. A narrator can be the writer but may also be a character in the story.
narrative	=	a name for the account of events given in a book, a play or a poem.
open questions	=	questions for which there is more than one answer and where a person has to think before replying. Questions that begin, 'What do you think about...?' are open questions.
paragraph	=	a group of sentences that are linked together by their meaning. Paragraphs often start with their first word slightly indented. Otherwise there is often a blank line between paragraphs.

Glossary

The word		What it means
parody	=	an imitation of a story, play or poem that makes fun of it by mocking or exaggerating some of its features or by playing on its weaknesses.
phrase	=	a group of words that are connected but do not make sense on their own.
plot	=	the main events in a story. The plot of a story is often used to summarise that story.
point size	=	a way of measuring the size of a typface. Headlines are often as big as 60pt type but this glossary is written in 8pt. Bigger typefaces are easier to read but they take up more space on the page.
presentation	=	the features of layout, neat handwriting and spelling that make writing attractive and easy to read so that it communicates its message more effectively.
proof-read	=	a final check on writing, for punctuation and spelling errors
question mark	=	the punctuation mark (?) that shows when the preceding phrase is asking a question. In reading aloud, a question mark can change the way that a sentence is spoken.
quotation	=	lines from another writer that are included in writing. Quotation marks are usually single for 'titles' and single words. Double "quotation" marks are used for direct speech and for longer extracts.
rhythm	=	the regular beat of the words in poetry or rhyme. Rhythm is created by the patterns of sounds in a word.
role play	=	improvising a scene, where each person plays a particular part, or role, and tries to react as the person they are playing would if he or she was in that situation.
scene	=	part of a play set in one place and at one time. A new scene starts when either the time or the place alters.
script	=	writing in play form. The writing is set out so that it can be acted or read by a number of people. It includes descriptions of the stage, entrances and exits and of how things should be said. TV, film and radio scripts have this sort of layout with minor variations.
sentence	=	a group of words which make sense when written on their own. Sentences begin with a capital letter and end with a full stop, a question mark or an exclamation mark.
setting	=	the background to a play or story. In a playscript, this could be a few words; in a novel several pages.
simile	=	a very common form of comparison which uses the words 'like' or 'as'.
slang	=	the use of informal words, bad language or shortened words in speech or writing. Often, slang has its own rules or its own vocabulary.
stage directions	=	the instructions (often in brackets or italics) in a playscript. They describe the background, the things that are on the stage, the times when characters should enter and leave and, often, how they should look.
standard English	=	the dialect of English that is accepted as the correct form for writing. People who speak a regional dialect at home often speak standard English in formal situations.

The word		What it means
structure	=	the shape or framework of a piece of writing. Well-structured writing makes more sense to a reader.
style	=	a way of describing the collected features of a piece of writing – the choice of words, the length of sentences, the use of direct speech or specialist language. The style of a piece of writing can be formal or informal, old-fashioned or modern, detailed and descriptive, or bare.
sub-plot	=	events in a play or story that run alongside the main story. A sub-plot can provide extra drama and excitement, some comic relief or show how things might have turned out differently for the characters.
summary	=	a shortened version of a piece of writing that has the same structure as the original but cuts out unnecessary detail.
syntax	=	how words are ordered in a language into sentences. As an example, in English, syntax says that adjectives usually go in front of nouns. The syntax in French says they should usually go after.
theme	=	an idea, a belief or a moral that runs through a story, play or poem.
typeface	=	the shape of the letters used in print. The typefaces used by word processors are known as 'fonts'.
upper case	=	CAPITAL letters – often used for effect or for titles and headings.
viewpoint	=	a way of describing how different characters in a story may see what happens differently.

Acknowledgements

We are grateful to the following for permission to reproduce photographs:

Associated Press page 8; The British Broadcasting Company page 70; The British Library pages 26, 27; The British Turkey Information Centre page 132; The Central Office of Information page 115; Central Television page 70; The Environmental Picture Library pages 30, 126 (© Vanessa Miles), 134 (© Patrick Sutherland); Mary Evans pages 26 (left and right), 31, 43, 55; Eye Ubiquitous page 90 (centre © Paul Stuart); The Folger Shakespeare Library page 55 (bottom, 56); Gazelian Photograph page 124 (© Justin Slee); Sally and Richard Greenhill page 102; David Hoffman pages 118–9; James Barlow/Impact Photo Library page 137; Jarrold Publishing page 55 (right); Chris Locke Graphics page 55; The Kobal Collection pages 70, 90 (top); Rex Features Ltd pages 90 (bottom © Jay David Buchsbaum), 114, 125; Ernest H Shepard and Methuen Children's Books pages 24, 29; Thames Television page 70; World Society for the Protection of Animals page 128; Zefa page 46.

All other photographs by Longman Photographic Unit.

We are grateful to the following for permission to reproduce copyright material:

Edinburgh University Press for the rap 'Men Talk' by Liz Lochhead from **True Confessions** 1985; The Guardian for an extract from the article 'Deadly Consequences' in **Education Guardian** 02/02/93; Haytul Pty Ltd c/o Curtis Brown (Aust) Pty Ltd, Sydney, for the poem 'Thank you Letter' by Robin Klein for **Snakes and Ladders**; the author's agents on behalf of Felice Holman for the poem 'Supermarket' from **At the Top of My Voice** and Other Poems by Felice Holman, published by Charles Scribner's Sons. © 1970 by Felice Holman; Penguin Books Ltd for 'Calligram' (15 May 1915, p77) from **Selected Poems** by Apollinaire, translated by Oliver Bernard (Penguin Books 1965), translation copyright © Oliver Bernard, 1965; the author, V.N. Petty for his poem 'Breakfast'; Second Wave for 'When Last I Did See You' by Liselle Kayla extracted from the anthology **Dead Proud** edited by Ann Considine & Robyn Slovo; author's agents on behalf of the late Dylan Thomas for 'In the Spin' from Collected Poems. pubd. J.M. Dent & Sons Ltd.

We have been unable to trace the copyright holders of the extract from **Murder in Cornwall** by Gloria Cook, poems 'Breathless' by Wilfred Noyce, 'Friendly Warning' by Robert Froman, 'Short Story' by David R. Morgan, extracts 'The Harry Hastings Method' by Warner Law, 'The Red Ball' by Ismith Khan, 'Windigo' by Sylvia Mark, 'Zoo Cage' by Michael Rosen and an extract from 'Canterbury Tales' by Geoffrey Chaucer, translated by Nevill Coghill, and would appreciate any information which would enable us to do so.

Every effort has been made to trace and acknowledge ownership of copyright. The publishers will be glad to make suitable arrangements with any copyright holders who it has not been possible to contact.